The Survival Guide

Unlocking the Power of the Trinity

Author: Damian C. Stewart

Published in Philadelphia, Pennsylvania by Damian C. Stewart

Cover Design: Damian C. Stewart

Library of Congress

LCCN: 2020925061

ISBN: 978-1-7365643-1-8 (Paperback)

CONTACT INFORMATION:

Pastor Damian C. Stewart

Pastordcstewart@gmail.com

Printed in the United States of America

DEDICATION

This book is dedicated to my parents
Charles E. Stewart and Sharon M. Stewart.
I am forever in debt to God for granting me the honor and advantage of being raised by two individuals whose love and fear of Him have provided me with a sound Biblical foundation.

INTRODUCTION

I would like to welcome you to this 165-page journey to unlocking the power of the Trinity in our lives. What will this journey entail? The best way for me to answer this question is to tell you what not to expect from reading this book. This book is not designed to answer all the questions you have about God or prove any person or group to be right or wrong. The purpose of this book is to enhance your knowledge of how the Trinity operates in the life of a believer to help you maximize living life abundantly with God. Prayerfully this this book will be a tool to help develop your maturing relationship with God by fortifying your foundational understanding.

When considering the durability of a built structure such as a home, school or an office building, the unseen foundation directly impacts or effects the durability of the exposed or seen portion of the structure. Over the course of time, the visible portion above ground will experience 'wear and tear', due to weather conditions and the process of settling. The structures ability to remain intact and habitable through all the changes is greatly determined by **the quality and durability of the foundation.** The portion of the structure above ground is what we furnish, make cosmetic changes to, entertain in and actually occupy. We enjoy ourselves in the portion of the structure above ground without any clue or knowledge of what is happening in the unseen portion of the structure underground, the foundation we built upon. Over the course of time, we may notice a crack, hinting at a potential problem that is often dismissed or ignored. We regard the potential danger as just being "a little crack", and move on with our regular routine. We do this not fully understanding the potential danger worsening with time, thus we ignore and continue use of the structure. A **faulty foundation** does not have an immediate devastating effect, but over the course of time it can cause the structure to become hazardous or condemned, making the structure uninhabitable. All the effort and cost to decorate, custom furnish and pay off the mortgage, becomes all for naught. The occupant or those who benefitted from the structure now find themselves in need of something new.

Spiritually, when we consider dealing with a faulty foundation, it has the same potential as the natural case scenario. The concept of God we build our foundation upon guides our perceptions and conclusions. Our perceptions and conclusions directly impact the development of a healthy relationship with God. It is possible for an individual to be totally unaware that certain aspects of their foundational knowledge and understanding of God contain faulty doctrines. The word doctrine is defined in Wikipedia as a codification of beliefs or a body of teachings of instructions, taught principles, or positions, as the essence of teachings in a given branch of knowledge or in a belief system. Embracing a faulty doctrine in ignorance has the potential to position us to make decisions detrimental to our future progression. Over the course of time the spiritual outcome mirrors that of a natural building with a faulty foundation. What we have built and established may be rendered hazardous and condemned, thus having to be totally demolished or go through several structure modifications. This causes us to vacate or abandon what we have built, requiring us to start from scratch or dismiss a large portion of what we have adapted our lives to. Thus, our beliefs, relationships, habits, etc. are all affected.

Dealing with a faulty foundation is a monumental undertaking and our willingness to take on such a project differs. On the 'A' end of the spectrum are those who consider it too costly to repair the faulty foundation; they examine what it will take to repair and fortify their foundational knowledge and understanding of God and determine the repairs to be too time consuming. As a result, this group opts to live their lives without God as a critical factor and resolve to live life void of any concrete, finalized or concluded thought of God. On total opposite 'Z' end of the spectrum are those who immediately begin repairing the breach once they become aware that their foundational knowledge and understanding of God includes faulty doctrine. These individuals engage in efforts to repair and fortify their knowledge and understanding of God. Between 'A' and 'Z' are a full-range of people who lean toward one end or the other.

One of the greatest mysteries pertaining to understanding God today is The Trinity or God in three. I believe The Trinity is one of the most misconstrued and ill-explained aspects of God. Yet it is the cornerstone to understanding God in His fullness. A believer's understanding of The Trinity is a key component to establishing and developing a maturing relationship with God.

I am honored God inspired me to write this book. My continued prayer is that the information contained within will empower believers to grow in their knowledge and understanding of God by helping to fortify a doctrinally sound foundation. Increased knowledge and understanding will prayerfully cause readers to not just have life, but "have it more abundantly". (John 10:10).

TABLE OF CONTENTS

We will now move forward in our journey to establish how we are here **by the will of the Father**, able to reconnect to the Father **because of** the sacrifice of **the Son** and able to enjoy life **with** the guidance of the **Holy Spirit.**

Before we continue, I request that you pray and ask God to grant you knowledge and understanding to arrive at wise deductions regarding His truth every time you read this book.

CHAPTER 1

Defining the Trinity

What a better way to embark upon our journey together than to ask a few questions. Who is God? What is God? How does God function? How our minds processed answering these questions allows most of us to fit into one of the following groups:

- Group A - Your mind started a mental search accessing all the information you have learned, been exposed to, or experienced. After assessing the information, you began eliminating any information you deemed unimportant or not 100% trustworthy to arrive at the most intelligent answer.
- Group B - Without hesitation your mind went on a one-way destination to the preconceived concluded answer you have already settled on. This definition of God is solidified in your mind and it is what you live according to.

- Group C – Your mind immediately dismissed the questions for various reasons.

It always amazes me what these questions trigger in people, even Christians (believers of God through Christ). It would seem that Christians would have a unified answer to these questions, allowing them to respond swiftly and without hesitation. However, this is rarely the case. Is there one right answer as opposed to several possible acceptable answers? Is it possible for us to maximize our journey through life lacking a definite answer to these questions? Does not knowing the answer to the questions handicap or limit the way we live?

When I use the term God, I believe it allows me to communicate with all the components of the 'God-head' or the Trinity, without the need to refer to God the Father, Jesus Christ the son, or the Holy Spirit independently. However, I also believe it is essential to understand that the function of the God the Father, Jesus Christ the Son, and the Holy Spirit in my life are not the same. As we journey through this book, we will explore each aspect of the Trinity. I want to note at the onset of our journey that while the Father, Son and Holy Spirit work in concert, the Son and the Holy Spirit are subject, led or controlled by the Father. Jesus Christ the son of God represents the physical manifestation of the

Word of God. *Christ executed and executes the will of the Father. The Holy Spirit* is the empowering transferable or projectable essence of God that *conveys the will of the Father.* Again, I believe the Father, the Son and the Holy Spirit are three different entities that function as one. Knowing how each aspect of Trinity is designed to effect and affect our lives affords us the opportunity to properly approach, communicate and set expectations—and not be in violation due to ignorance.

CHAPTER 2

God, the Father

2.1: THE CREATOR AND ARCHITECT

Let us examine the role and preeminence of the Father in the Trinity and to creation. Human nature often causes us to understand or translate definitions through our personal experience. Based upon this, the word or term father can limit our full understanding and comprehension of God our Heavenly Father. Varying personal experiences can cause the exact meaning of the word father to potentially hinder and limit agreement. As we consider God the Father and our primary relationship to Him, for this chapter I request we transition our view from God the Father, to God the Creator and Architect, Elohim the One who is power and strength. As the Creator and Architect, God has rule of the Heavens & the Earth and they dwell within it. Let us explore a few definitions provided by Dictionary.com.

1. Father – a male who exercises paternal care over other persons; paternal protector or provider.
2. Creator - to cause to happen, bring about; arrange as by intention of design.
3. Architect - one who plans, organizes, or structures.

The duty of an **architect** is to know the end purpose of what is being created, to assure the design is inclusive of all the intended uses. In the planning stages, an experienced architect includes utility lines (ways of getting needed resources), waste lines (providing a means to emit what is not wanted or harmful), safety precautions and emergency exits to provide alternative ways of escape in the event of an unwanted or unexpected occurrence. The completed final design protects both the building and the end user.

We must always remember, know and understand that God created 'it all' and He made certain 'it all' would work together in a 'fail-proof' fashion. 'It all' includes man. Let us explore scriptures that support viewing God as the Creator and Architect:

Genesis 1:1-2

In the beginning God created the heavens and the Earth. [2] Now the earth was formless and empty, darkness was over the surface of the deep, and the Spirit of God was hovering over the waters.

Genesis 1:26

Then God said, "Let Us make man in Our image, according to Our likeness…"

Psalms 24:1 - (Old Testament)

The Earth is the Lord's and the fullness of it, the world and they who dwell in it

I Corinthians 10:26 – (New Testament)

For "the earth is the Lord's and all its fullness"

Genesis 2:7

And the Lord God formed man of the dust of the ground, and breathed into his nostrils the breath of life; and man became a living being.

Exodus 3:13

[13] *Then Moses said to God, "Indeed, when I come to the children of Israel and say to them, 'The God of your fathers has sent me to you,' and they say to me, 'What is His name?' what shall I say to them?"* [14] *And God said to Moses, "I AM WHO I AM." And He said, "Thus you shall say to the children of Israel, 'I AM has sent me to you.'"* [15] *Moreover God said to Moses, "Thus you shall say to the children of Israel: 'The LORD God of your fathers, the God of Abraham, the God of Isaac, and the God of Jacob, has sent me to you. This is My name forever, and this is My memorial to all generations.'*

<u>Job 38:1-7</u>

Then the LORD answered Job out of the whirlwind, and said: [2] "Who is this who darkens counsel by words without knowledge? [3] Now prepare yourself like a man; I will question you, and you shall answer Me. [4] "Where were you when I laid the foundations of the earth? Tell Me, if you have understanding. [5] Who determined its measurements? Surely you know! Or who stretched the line upon it? [6] To what were its foundations fastened? Or who laid its cornerstone, [7] When the morning stars sang together, and all the sons of God shouted for joy?

Prayerfully these scriptures have allowed you to be in agreement with my request to refer to God as Creator and Architect.

2.2: GAINING THE RIGHT PERSPECTIVE AND POSITION

Understanding the Father as the **Creator** and **Architect** is crucial to how we perceive life and function within it. Gaining this vantage point, directly impacts our **level of submission to God** and correlates to **how we experience God**. God will use us according to His pleasure and purpose whether we take the position of being a vessel of honor or dishonor, whether we agree or oppose. In the above passage from Job, God was simply reminding Job who he was in the 'scheme of things' vs. who He (God) was, is and yet will be.

Job was offered up by God to the Devil. God even heeded the Devil's challenge to lift the protections afforded to Job. Job didn't do anything wrong; he was offered up because of what he had done right. As Creator and Architect it is God's right to use us however He determines best. While Job's statement, "the Lord giveth and the Lord taketh away", allows us to understand that he grasped the concept of being a pawn on God's chess board, his attitude toward God shifted after his family, wealth and health was touched. It shifted in a way that caused God to 'put Job in His place'. Surely, God understood the gravity of how His allowance would and could affect Job. Surely! I believe his 'putting Job in His place' was His way of assuring Job did not lose His place and future reward by letting his emotions reposition Him in the God-initiated storm. We must be careful to watch how we let our turbulent times affect our level of reverence for God. God does not have a problem with us asking Him questions, but I believe how we ask Him can become extremely problematic. Let us consider these two scriptures, to make certain we have the proper starting position as we relate to God the Creator and Architect:

Romans 9:20

[20] *But indeed, O man, who are you to reply against God? Will the thing formed say to him who formed it, "Why have you made me like this?"*

Proverbs 1:7

The fear of the LORD is the beginning of knowledge,
But fools despise wisdom and instruction.

Proverbs 9:9-10

[10] *"The fear of the LORD is the beginning of wisdom,*

and the knowledge of the Holy One is understanding.
[11] *For by me your days will be multiplied, and years of life will be added to you.*

Our level of submission makes us assume a posture of acceptance or rejection, as it pertains to what God wills or allows to be. While undoubtedly God is loving and merciful, we are admonished in Proverbs that the fear of the Lord, not the love of Lord, is the beginning of wisdom. The fear of the Lord keeps us in the correct position for what he allows life to throw our way. It keeps us ready for use when we don't understand and when we don't' agree. Do you believe you are in the right mindset to be used by God, even in the most challenging times? Was your starting point of submission in alignment with the wisdom revealed in Proverbs 1:7 and Proverbs 9:10? **We will either flow with God or take the position of being against Him.** God the Father, the Creator and Architect, The I Am, is the 'Driving Force' of the Trinity. It is important that we understand that God the Creator and Architect is also the 'Course Setter' for all activity on the Earth. This has great significance on *how* and what we communicate to God our Creator and Architect. Let us enlist the following key scriptures to help us develop the correct mindset concerning this:

Ecclesiastes 3:1

To everything there is a season,
A time for every purpose under heaven: [11] *He has made everything beautiful in its time. Also He has put eternity in their hearts, except that no one can find out the work that God does from beginning to end.*

Isaiah 46:9-13

Remember the former things of old, for I am God, and there is no other; I am God, and there is none like Me, [10] *Declaring the end from the beginning, And from ancient times things that are not yet done, Saying, 'My counsel shall stand, And I will do all My pleasure,* [11] *Calling a bird of prey from the east, The man who executes My counsel, from a far country. Indeed I have spoken it; I will also bring it to pass. I have purposed it; I will also do it.*

Isaiah 55:8-11

"For My thoughts are not your thoughts, nor are your ways My ways," says the LORD. [9] *"For as the heavens are higher than the earth, so are My ways higher than your ways, and My thoughts than your thoughts.* [10] *"For as the rain comes down, and the snow from heaven, And do not return there, but water the earth, and make it bring forth and bud, That it may give seed to the sower and bread to the eater,* [11] *So shall My word be that goes forth from My mouth; It shall not return to Me void, But it shall accomplish what I please, And it shall prosper in the thing for which I sent it.*

I Corinthians 1:25-30

[25] Because the foolishness of God is wiser than men, and the weakness of God is stronger than men. [26] For you see your calling, brethren, that not many wise according to the flesh, not many mighty, not many noble, are called. [27] But God has chosen the foolish things of the world to put to shame the wise, and God has chosen the weak things of the world to put to shame the things which are mighty; [28] and the base things of the world and the things which are despised God has chosen, and the things which are not, to bring to nothing the things that are, [29] that no flesh should glory in His presence. [30] But of Him you are in Christ Jesus, who became for us wisdom from God – and righteousness and sanctification and redemption –

Hebrews 11:3

[3] By faith we understand that the worlds were framed by the word of God, so that the things which are seen were not made of things which are visible.

These scriptures lay a solid foundation for us to fully grasp, comprehend and accept God as the Creator and Architect. Our Creator has a plan for the Earth and humanity. God's plan must be fulfilled. What is His plan? What part do you and I play within His plan? God's ways are not our ways, nor are His thoughts our thoughts. This means God has a deliberate and intentional habit of using the foolish things of the world to confound the wise. Based on this truth, we are not capable of figuring out how He will execute His plan and **are rendered incapable of receiving these answers independent of God**. Our Creator is the only one capable of leading us to the correct answers pertaining to the Earth and ourselves. We must never forget God assigned the management of Earth to mankind, thus He moves through man in the Earth realm. God does not give mankind (you and I) the option to choose if we will go along with His plan, but He does give us the option of how we will live within His plan. Will we choose to be a vessel of honor or dishonor?

God designed you and I based on His purpose, He implanted gifts within us based upon our assignment within His purpose. Therefore seeking God's mind tremendously beneficial to us. Knowing God's mind empowers us to know our role within His overarching purpose. **Known purpose helps assure we are in alignment with God and not in violation.**

Think of a well-designed building, bridge and video game. I recall viewing many buildings in awe, driving over bridges in amazement. I also remember playing a video game wondering who sat down and thought about all the intricate details of each level. In each case, someone took the time needed to conceptualize it being a possibility and developed a plan to allow the intangible concept to materialize into becoming a tangible and useable reality. Again, please think about a building you have seen, a bridge you have driven over, or a complicated video game you have played. Would you want to be on the top floor of the building based upon your knowledge to design it? Would you want to drive over a bridge based upon your knowledge of how to assure its safety? Would you be eager to play a video game based upon your knowledge of how to program it and comprise the illustrative images on each differing level? For me, the answer to all three is a resounding "no." We depend on individuals with the knowledge, understanding, training and experience to make the things we use safe and exciting. Now if a human being can achieve these things, what is the all-powerful, all-knowing, omnipresent God capable of planning and executing?

What is God's level of thinking, operation and capability to produce? I believe God created a system capable of guaranteeing the manifestation and execution of His will, without the need of His involvement, but not void of His intervention. I believe we are witnessing and living within this system daily.

2.3: EXPANDING OUR VIEW OF THE FATHER

This particular segment is one that I debated 'touching on' at all or at this particular point in the book. After careful thought, I concluded that in order for our minds to open to the fullness of the Trinity, and how we perceive God, we should explore the question, "How does the Father exist, or in what form?" I was raised in a Pentecostal Church and have heard many explanations or references to how God the Father exists. After careful thought, study, evaluation of theories, etc., my position probably challenges being in alignment with mainstream Pentecostal theories and general assumptions.

To provide a solid foundation let us establish the difference between fact and theory. Wikipedia defines the word fact as a statement that is consistent with objective reality or can be proven with evidence. Another definition is a thing that is indisputably the case. There are certain things contained within scripture that are factually based on what is written in the Bible. A few examples are:

- ✓ Jesus Christ is the son of God.
- ✓ Love is the greatest gift of all.
- ✓ God judges a man by his heart, not his outward appearance.
- ✓ God created Earth.

Each of the statements above can be confirmed through scripture references in a manner that establishes them as undebatable facts. A theory is different. Businessdictionary.com defines the word theory as a set of assumptions, propositions (suggestions), or accepted facts that attempts to provide a plausible (credible, possible) or rational (sensible, logical) explanation of cause-and-effect (causal) relationships among a group of observed phenomenon (facts). The word's origin (from the Greek thorós, a spectator) stresses the fact that all theories are mental models of the perceived reality. In short, a well-founded, plausible justifiable or valid theory is an explanation derived from multiple facts. However, no matter how well thought out a theory is, it will remain a theory until it is proven or substantiated beyond question.

The prevailing theory I have heard regarding how God, the Father exists, is that He is not physically tangible, because He is Spirit. This theory is primarily derived from the following scripture in the Gospel of John:

John 4:23-25

[23] *But the hour is coming, and now is, when the true worshipers will worship the Father in spirit and truth; for the Father is seeking such to worship Him.* [24] ***God is Spirit, and those who worship Him must worship in spirit and truth.***"

In brief, I believe viewing God as an intangible Spirit Being, limits our scope of His existence and operation. It is my theory that God, the Father has physical form and this physical form is independent of His son Jesus Christ. My belief does not mean I do not embrace the truth revealed in John 4:23-25, I fully believe it. However, I believe the spirit realm has tangible physical beings, including the Father. In John 4:23-25 we are advised that God is Spirit and those who worship Him must worship in spirit and truth. My interpretation of this text is that in our sin-filled flesh we are incapable of physically connecting with God. However, we are granted access to connect with God in the Spirit realm through the gift of His Holy Spirit that dwells inside every believer. A few of scriptures that led to my belief of God the Father existing in tangible physical form, in the spirit realm are:

Genesis 3:8

And they heard the voice of the LORD God walking in the garden in the cool of the day: and Adam and his wife hid themselves from the presence of the LORD God amongst the trees of the garden.

Psalms 110:1

The LORD said to my Lord, Sit thou at my right hand, until I make thine enemies thy footstool.

Revelation 21

And ***I saw a new heaven and a new earth****: for the first heaven and the first earth were passed away; and there was no more sea.* [2] *And I John saw the holy city, new Jerusalem, coming down from God out of heaven, prepared as a bride adorned for her husband.* [3] ***And I heard a great voice out of heaven saying, Behold, the tabernacle of God is with men, and He will dwell with them, and they shall be His people, and God himself shall be with them, and be their God.*** [4] *And God shall wipe away all tears from their eyes; and there shall be no more death, neither sorrow, nor crying, neither shall there be any more pain: for the former things are passed away.* [5] *And He that sat upon the throne said, Behold, I make all things new. And he said unto me, Write: for these words are true and faithful.* [6] *And he said unto me, It is done. I am Alpha and Omega, the beginning and the end. I will give unto him that is athirst of the fountain of the water of life freely.*

In upcoming chapters I will give a more detailed explanation about the significance of these scriptures, but for now, I believe:

1. God, the Father, Creator and Architect was physically walking in the Garden of Eden in Genesis chapter 3.
2. God the Father is saying to His Son, take rest and sit here at my right hand until the appointed time (the second coming) in Psalms 110. What need is there for the Father to have a throne if he did not exist in physical form?
3. From Revelation chapter 21, the description of God leads me to believe the Father's intent is to actually dwell with mankind, after the second coming of Christ. I do not interpret this to be an inward dwelling. I believe this speaks to God in physical form existing with us.
4. I do not subscribe or believe in the Christophany Theory or the theory that every time God is believed to walk among man in scripture, He takes the form of a pre-incarnate Christ.

Please remember, while it comes from me it remains a theory and not a fact. Now let's move forward and dive into the Father being the leader to the Trinity.

2.4: THE LEADER OF THE TRINITY

The concept of God in three or The Trinity is so complex based on our human experience that most people do not seek a clear understanding. Our attempt to conceptualize the fullness of the Trinity by mere human intellect is limited due to it being shaped by earthly experiences and facts. We are incapable of fully understanding many aspects of God independent of His guidance; it requires the illumination of the Holy Spirit. This is why I advised readers (page 6) to pray and ask God to be granted knowledge and understanding as they read this book. Without God's guidance, understanding Him becomes a limited, frustrating, or fruitless mission. An individual's knowledge of scripture is merely what they committed to memory; it does not equate to their depth of understanding, if any at all. Likewise, our knowledge and understanding of scripture does not guarantee our decisions have or will reflect the proper application of what we know and understand. I believe wisdom as exhibited by mankind, is the proper of application of knowledge and understanding.

To help us build on what we know of the Trinity and increase our level of understanding, let's look at John the Revelator's description of the throne of God:

Revelations 1:4-6

Grace to you and peace from [1] Him who is and who was and who is to come (the Father), and from [2] the seven Spirits who are before His throne (The Holy Spirit), [5] and from [3] Jesus Christ, the faithful witness, the firstborn from the dead, and the ruler over the kings of the earth. To Him who loved us and washed[a] us from our sins in His own blood (the Son), [6] and has made us kings[b] and priests to His God and Father, to Him be glory and dominion forever and ever. Amen.

The Collins English Dictionary defines the prefix 'tri' as having, combining, or involving three. In this text John is given the opportunity to see the throne of God, the dwelling place of the Trinity. John's description is detailed. He references seeing each part of the Trinity separately, the Father, the seven fold Holy Spirit and Jesus Christ the Son. This helps confirm that the Father and the Son exist as separate entities. To help support my theory let us examine Stephen's and David reference:

Acts 7:55-56

[55] But he (Stephen), being full of the Holy Spirit, gazed into heaven and saw the glory of God, and Jesus standing at the right hand of God, [56] and said, "Look! I see the heavens opened and the Son of Man standing at the right hand of God!"

Mark 16:19

[19] So then, after the Lord had spoken to them, He was received up into heaven, and sat down at the right hand of God.

Psalms 110:1

The Lord (the Father) said to my Lord (Jesus Christ), "Sit at my right hand, till I make your enemies your footstool.

Hopefully, you accept these scripture references as evidence that God the Father and God the Son are one not entity, while they function in unity as one. The Father, Son and Holy Spirit work in total agreement. I would like to emphasize that the Father is the leader or the dominant of the three. It is the total obedience of Jesus Christ, which caused and causes Him to act as one with the Father. In the text below, we will read instances where Christ acknowledges that are somethings only the Father knows, and neither he nor other Heavenly beings have been given full disclosure. **It is the will of the Son (Jesus Christ) to**

execute, satisfy and fulfill the will of the Father. Let's get confirmation from Christ himself:

Mark 13:32

[32] *"But of that day and hour (referring to Christ second return to Earth) no one knows, not even the angels in heaven, nor the Son, but only the Father.*

John 8:28-29

[28] *Then Jesus said to them, "When you lift up the Son of Man, then you will know that I am He, and that I do nothing of Myself; but as My Father taught Me, I speak these things.* [29] *And He who sent Me is with Me. The Father has not left Me alone, for I always do those things that please Him."*

John 7:16

[16] *Jesus answered them and said, "My doctrine is not Mine, but His who sent Me.*

Christ also testifies or sheds light on the function and limitations of the Holy Spirit:

John 16:13

[13] *However, when He, the Spirit of truth, has come, He will guide you into all truth; for He will not speak on His own authority, but*

whatever He hears He will speak; and He will tell you things to come.

This is no way lessons or diminishes the significance of Jesus Christ or the Holy Spirit. Hopefully, it helps set the foundation for our understanding of the Trinity. Understanding the Trinity positions us to serve, reference and expect from God differently.

2.4: THE FATHER AND HIS WORD

What value do you place on a person being a man or woman of their word? How happy and overjoyed are you when someone follows through on what they promised? On the flipside of things, how disappointed or angry are you when someone does not honor their word? I am not sure what value you place on an individual's being true to their word, but it is high up on the Richter Scale for me. One of the main ways I judge an individual's character, believability and trustworthiness, is directly tied to them being a person of their word.

Our society places great emphasis on an individual being true to their word. Court cases are won or lost based upon a lawyer's ability to get a group of jurors to either believe a person's word or by disproving their word. Lawyers present information to sway the jury in favor of their client. Trials involve two opposing forces that are given the opportunity to each present evidence in hopes of convincing the jurors of the truth they are presenting. In a defense case, where a defendant is involved, if the defendant's lawyer is successful at manufacturing even a shadow of doubt, the person on trial is supposed to be set free, because the 'law of the land' states the person must be proven guilty beyond a "shadow of doubt".

The Bible teaches that God is serious about people honoring their word. He places a great deal of weight on His Word as well. God magnifies His Word above His name, He places more emphasis on His Word than His identity or what He's known to be. This means God revers, exalts and is committed His Word. God will not go against His Word, while He is fully able to. We should celebrate this factual truth daily! Let's qualify this:

Psalms 138:2

I will worship toward Your holy temple, And praise Your name For Your lovingkindness and Your truth; For You have magnified Your word above all Your name.

Numbers 23:19 –

"God is not a man, that He should lie, nor a son of man, that He should repent. Has He said, and will He not do? Or has He spoken, and will He not make it good?

In simple terms, God stakes being true to his Word on everything He is. He is committed to deliver on what He promises, establishes, sets in order, etc. If this be true, God is limited by His Word. He confines Himself to work within the parameters of what His Word framed. Let's consider the value of word through the lens of John:

John 1:1-3

In the beginning was the word, and the word was with God and the word was God. He was God in the beginning. All things were made through Him, and without Him nothing was made that was made.

So, God has been one with His Word from the beginning of time. Everything that God created on Earth was manifested by Him speaking it into existence, or by His Word, excluding man. This gives special importance to the use of words by God, as it relates to His purpose for mankind and how methodical (systematic, precise, disciplined) our Creator was in executing His will for Earth and all that would come to exist within it.

In the Merriam Webster Dictionary 'word' is defined as a speech sound or series of speech sounds that symbolizes and communicates a meaning usually without being divisible into smaller units capable of independent use. In

Greek 'Word' is translated from the Greek term *logos* meaning spoken or unspoken word. The Collins Dictionary defines *logos* as the reason or rational principle expressed in words and things, argument, or justification; especially personified as the source of order in the universe. The Zondervan All-In-One Reference Guide defines *logos (word)* as the dynamic principle of reason operating in the world and forming a medium (standard) of communion between God and man. Moving forward let's use the following definition to explain God's Word: **the rational principle that governs (directs, manages or controls) all things. So, let's now insert the definition into the text**:

John 1:1-2

In the beginning was ***the rational principle that governs all things****, the* ***rational principle that governs all things*** *was with God, and* ***the rational principle that governs all things*** *was God. He (God, the Creator) was God in the beginning.*

Please note that 'erns' is underlined in the word governs. I want to emphasis here the implication or meaning of governs is that it continues to be, or it hasn't ceased.

It is my belief that the intent of the text is to reveal what governed and governs God in all things. What was present in the beginning to be God's point of reference?

What was with God and what was God? It is my theory that the answers to these questions lead us to understand or conclude that **God, the Creator's spoken Word is** synonymous to, parallel with, or equivalent to **His concluded thought, end thought or purpose revealed**. God enlists the Holy Spirit to carry out aspects of His purpose, so Proverbs chapters eight and nine can also be interpreted as a 'heartfelt' expression of the Holy Spirit. We read about this aspect more in the chapters that deal with the Holy Spirit. For now, with God's Word being synonymous with His purpose revealed, I believe what governs God is His purpose, and His purpose can be found in His Word (The Bible). Let's look at the following passage and insert the word purpose to support my theory:

Proverbs 8:22

The Lord possessed (purposed) me at the beginning of His way, before His works of old. [23] I (purpose) have been established from everlasting, from the beginning, before there was ever an earth. [30] Then I (purpose, His spoken Word) was beside Him as a master craftsman; and I was daily His delight, rejoicing always before Him, rejoicing in His inhabited world, ***and my delight was with the sons of men****. [32] Now therefore, listen to me (purpose revealed, His spoken word), my children, for blessed (esher = how happy) are those who keep my ways. [33] Hear instruction and be wise, and do not disdain it. [34] Blessed is the* *man who listens to me (God's purpose), watching daily at my gates, waiting at the posts of my doors. [35] For whoever finds me (purpose, God's concluded thought) finds life, and obtains favor from the Lord; [36] But he who sins against me (purpose) wrongs his own soul; all those who hate me (purpose, God's word) love death. (NKJV)*

God our Creator and Architect (the Father) is one with His Word. Previously, I believed the goal of John 1:1-3 was to highlight and point out distinctions between God and His Word. Now, I understand John 1:1-3 establishes and highlights the fact of God and His Word (the rational principle that governs God) are one. God, the Father governs Himself by His Word. I believe God established His Word to serve as the medium all creation would use to view or judge His character, goodness, consistency, dependability, etc. upon. The Creator and Architect of the Earth actually values our valid opinion regarding Him so much, that He will remain eternally committed to uphold and deliver based upon His Word (His end thought, or purpose revealed).

To really put this to test let's consider the relationship between a parent and a child. As a child grows, what their parents say, their words, form their child's entire world. A child learns, lives by, is controlled by and bases their expectations upon the words (advice, counsel, chastisement, praise, etc.) of their parents. However, as a child matures what a parent 'says' as it relates to what they 'do' causes the child to lose or gain respect, honor and reverence for their parents' word.

Like a child, our opinion of our Heavenly Father is based upon Him honoring His word (His concluded thought, promises and judgements) contained within the scriptures regarding the past, present and future. Knowing God's word or purpose allows us to gain a dependency on God, which forms correlating expectations of God. Knowing God's word provides the benefit of being able to plan based on Godly wisdom, which assures being in **divine alignment** vs. merely our common sense, which is an extremely limited perspective, rooted in what seems good. What is good from our perspective does not always equate to what is God; a good thing does not always equal a God thing. Not knowing the Word of God most assuredly will work against us. Being unaware of God's rational principle that is governing and at work in a situation we are experiencing is vital. Not knowing God's end thought or purpose revealed before we enter a situation can unknowingly position us against God, risking death. Ignorance has the potential to kill us.

An example of a good vs God idea can be found in the story of David bringing the Ark of the Covenant back to camp of God's people. In the book of II Samuel chapter 6, the Ark of the Covenant was not transported in the manner God prescribed. They transported the Ark on the back of animals instead of on the shoulders of man as mandated by God. This violation cost Uzzah his life. Uzzah was doing what he perceived as good, but he was ignorant to God's previous instruction regarding how to transport the Ark of the Covenant where His glory rested. God's instruction was for His glory (the Ark) never to be touched by man. He instructed that staves be placed in rings on the side for the purpose of transporting the Ark. While transporting the Ark an animal lost footing and the Ark began to tilt as to fall and Uzah reached out his hand in attempt to level the Ark of the Covenant and keep it from falling. This noble act caused God's wrath to broke out against Uzzah. God gave specific details on the Ark was to be handled, respected and transported. **Uzzah's best intentions and utmost respect for Ark of God were not enough to spare him from the consequences of not following the prescription or guidelines of God's Word**.

The Word of God is the foundation for what He created and framed and what He creates and frames. His Word reveals what He has done, is doing, will do, allows and prohibits. The text in Proverbs 8 empowers us to understand what is orchestrating our existence on Earth and upholding all within the Earth realm. God created in harmony with His purpose and when He spoke His concluded thought it was manifested. This is why the Word of God (the Bible, His purposed revealed) is so precious and important.

2.5: PARTNERSHIP WITH THE FATHER

God, the Creator and Architect (the Father) wants us to know 'what He's up to.' He wants us to know how to please Him and how to efficiently play our part in His plan. Wow! What an awesome opportunity to partner with the Creator and Architect by knowing His reasoning and His mind 'in-part.'

I Corinthians 13:9-12
[9] *For we know in part and we prophesy in part.*

John 15:15 (Jesus speaking to His disciples)
[15] *No longer do I call you servants, for a servant does not know what his master is doing; but I have called you friends, for all things that I heard from My Father I have made known to you.*

God grants us the opportunity to partner or operate within His will from a cooperative or submitted position; however we must rely on Him leading us to the knowledge and understanding available in every situation.

<u>Proverbs 3:5-7</u>

Trust in the LORD with all thine heart; and lean not unto thine own understanding. [6] In all thy ways acknowledge him, and he shall direct thy paths. [7] Be not wise in thine own eyes. Do not Fear the LORD and depart from evil.

<u>Psalms 119:105</u>

The Word of God is a lamp unto me feet and a light unto my path.

Each of us is granted differing levels of access based on many factors, including assignment (predestined purpose), having a foundation that will allow proper processing of information received, and the level of our submission and agreement to His will and way. One with a high level of access or revelation is undeniable. I would like to highlight that one's lifestyle does not necessarily dictate the level of access granted and associated power released. This fact makes evident that one's predestined assignment is a dominating factor. However, please note, with all we are able to learn and know, no one man or group of men will ever know the mind of God in its entirely. This is by God's design. Let's add a layer or two to strengthen our foundation about the importance knowing God's mind in matters:

I Corinthians 1:27

But God has chosen the foolish things of the world to put to shame the wise, and God has chosen the weak things of the world to put to shame the things which are mighty;

Isaiah 55:10-11

(God is speaking through the prophet Isaiah)

Before reading Isaiah 55:10-11, it is important to note the meaning of 'word' here is from the Hebrew word "dabar"(Strong's 1697) meaning a matter (as spoken of) or thing; or cause. From Strong's 1696, "dabar" meaning to arrange (figuratively speaking of words); to subdue (control)

[10]*For as the rain comes down, and the snow from heaven, and do not return there, but water the earth, and make it bring for the and bud, that it may give seed to the sower and bread to the eater,* ***so shall My Word*** *(matter, thing or cause) that goes forth from my mouth;* ***It shall will not return to Me void, but it*** *(God's concluded spoken thought or purpose)* ***shall accomplish what I please, and it shall prosper in the thing for which I sent it.*** *(NKJV)*

<u>Numbers 23:19</u>

"God is not a man, that He should lie, nor a son of man, that He should repent. Has ***He said, and will He not do****? Or has He spoken, and will He not make it good?*

Okay, let's pause and really let the power of God's Word sink in. God's purpose is synonymous with His perfect will. The **perfect will of God** is what he has ordained to be, his concluded thought spoken or His unalterable Word regarding a matter. The Perfect Will of God must accomplish what it was released to do, as emphasized by the preceding scriptures. With this in mind, in the next chapter we will explore living according to the perfect will of God.

2.6: THE CREATOR AND MANKIND

In previous chapters, emphasis was placed on the importance of shifting our mindset to viewing God as the Creator and Architect. God with a capital 'G' is translated from the Hebrew word *Elohim.* Elohim is defined as the supreme or ultimate reality; the Being perfect in power, wisdom and goodness who is worshipped as creator and ruler of the universe. If God is the **Creator**, as the scriptures reveal, then it is He who created or formed man. This makes us the **creation** of God and establishes a 'Creator to creation' relationship. Establishing who we are 'in the equation' empowers us to realize our true position as we relate to God. Relating to God from the right position enables us to gain a vantage point of submission. A position of submission will affect how we pursue, communicate, interpret and represent God. It enables us to maintain a posture of adherence to God's will independent of our agreement and understanding.

God gave man the authority to govern the Earth. God's directive to mankind was to be fruitful (be productive based on gifts instilled and resources available), multiply (have offspring), replenish (care for the Earth) and subdue the Earth (see the conditions in the Garden of Eden extended or expanded). Due to this, we must remember that God moves through man within the Earth realm to bring about His purpose. To accomplish achieving the assignment entrusted to us by God, we must submit to His instruction and be led by Him daily in every way. This is of vital importance because one wrong move can have devastating rippling affects. As the scripture in Proverbs revealed, we should be seeking God's will early in the day and waiting daily at the gates of God's purpose.

Let's go back and see how God set mankind up to govern. Man was the Father's final creation on Earth; everything else was created prior to man's existence. The Earth where man would serve and fulfill his purpose was prepared for him, independent of him. Everything man needed to survive and be sustained was thought of and given to him freely. Again, for man to know how to properly govern, tend to and advance what had been entrusted to him, connection to His Creator would be the requirement. Let explore these scriptures to verify:

Genesis 1:27-28; 2:15-17

So God created man in His own image; in the image of God He created him; male and female He created them. [28] Then God blessed them, and God said to them, "Be fruitful and multiply; fill the earth and subdue it; have dominion over the fish of the sea, over the birds of the air, and over every living thing that moves on the earth."

****(KJV) - [28] And God blessed them, and God said unto them, be fruitful, and multiply, **and replenish** the earth, and subdue it:*

2:15 -*Then the Lord God took the man and put him in the Garden of Eden to tend and keep it.* **[19]** *Out of the ground the LORD God formed every beast of the field and every bird of the air, and brought them to Adam to see what he would call them. And whatever Adam called each living creature, that was its name.* **[20]** *So Adam gave names to all cattle, to the birds of the air, and to every beast of the field.*

Psalms 37:23

[23] The steps of a good man are [b]ordered by the LORD, And He delights in his way. [24] Though he fall, he shall not be utterly cast down; For the LORD upholds him with His hand.

Proverbs 3:5-6

[5] Trust in the LORD with all your heart, and lean not on your own understanding; [6] In all your ways acknowledge Him, And He shall [a]direct your paths. [7] Do not be wise in your own eyes;

Proverbs 14:12

There is a way that seems right to a man, but its end is the way of death.

Knowledge of this helps us understand that God created mankind with predetermined purpose, clear intent and provision. From the above scriptures we ascertain that within God's overarching purpose (**the perfect will of God**), there also exist the **permissive will of God.** The instructions, boundaries and restrictions we receive from God, are designed to protect us in the area of God's permissive will. This initiates the need for mankind to trust God and be obedient to Him. Here are some scriptures to support the importance of seeking the mind of God and why obedience is vital to our existence and progression:

Isaiah 46:10

Declaring the end from the beginning, and from ancient times things that are not yet done, Saying, 'My counsel shall stand, And I will do all My pleasure,'

Isaiah 48:3

"I have declared the former things from the beginning; they went forth from My mouth, and I caused them to hear it. Suddenly I did them, and they came to pass. [5] Even from the beginning I have declared it to you; before it came to pass I proclaimed it to you, Lest you should say, 'My idol has done them, And my carved image and my molded image Have commanded them.'

Matthew 7:13-14

[13] *"Enter by the narrow gate; for wide is the gate and broad is the way that leads to destruction, and there are many who go in by it.* [14] [a]*Because narrow is the gate and* [b]*difficult is the way which leads to life, and there are few who find it.*

Matthew 6:33

[33] *But seek first the kingdom of God and His righteousness, and all these things shall be added to you.*

In our pursuit to learn and understand God, we would do well to have insight regarding how He thinks and plans. Scriptures reveal that God, the Creator and Architect (the Father) produces in accordance with His end goal or desire, meaning God plans from the end (determined purpose) to the beginning. **God arrives at His end desire and then provides for it**. Adam was placed in the Garden of Eden, which had perfect conditions for life. Adam only needed to tend and keep it, by following God's instructions. Adam was given guidelines of how to advance the conditions in the garden throughout the Earth (be fruitful, multiply, replenish and subdue). Adam was also advised what would bring about his demise. For you and I, communication with God helps us to know what God is 'up to' and what we're individually purposed to do within it.

We should seek to discover and develop the gifts God has instilled in us and the weapons He has made available to help us on the journey to fulfilling purpose. God is the source of all we need and He has a plan and correlating resources to equip us to abide in a position of victory. God advised Jeremiah that his purpose, associated authority and restrictions were placed upon him (Jeremiah), before he came forth from his mother's womb. God informed Jeremiah that he had called and sanctified him. Jeremiah was given a gift set based on his assignment. When Jeremiah tried to hold back operating in accordance with what he was purposed to due, he described the feeling to be likened to "fire shut up in his bones." However, could he really walk and be used in alignment with purpose without God's guiding Him? Like Jeremiah, you and I were also given a set of gifts and nothing we have done or can do will cause God to change His mind as advised in Romans 11:29.

Jeremiah 1:5

"Before I formed you in the womb I knew you; before you were born I sanctified you; I ordained you a prophet to the nations." [10] *See, I have this day set you over the nations and over the kingdoms, to root out and to pull down, to destroy and to throw down, to build and to plant."*

Romans 11:29

For the gifts and calling of God are without repentance.

Let's recap and add a layer. Man was God's 'crowning creation' on Earth and everything Adam needed was provided for him. God purposed mankind to have dominion and authority in Earth. Due to God making man the ruling authority on Earth, honoring His appointed commission, God moves through man to accomplish His purpose. This means in the event that we (mankind) violate the authority entrusted to us, or reject God's preferred path for us, He will not strip man of his authority. He doesn't have to; He fashioned the Earth to assure His purpose is fulfilled. As God's deputized agents in the Earth realm, we choose to fulfill our purpose as a vessel of honor or a vessel of dishonor. It is vital that we realize that people submitted to God (Christian disciples) are not the only individuals operating with power in the Earth realm. Both vessels of honor and dishonor exercise a level of authority in the Earth realm.

It appears that that vessels of dishonor, under the guidance of Satan, the fallen archangel Lucifer, understand how to work principles that will allow the gifts to flourish in the Earth realm. Remember, Satan is well aware of what the principles the Kingdom of God are built upon and regulated by. The Bible advises that God's own people are destroyed due to lack of knowledge or knowledge that is rejected. This truth highlights the importance of the work of the Holy Spirit that will be discussed in future chapters.

Here is the thing, mankind's ability to extend or reflect the Kingdom of God throughout the Earth is dependent upon our relationship with God being intact. Being in alignment with God allows us to fulfill our purpose with greater ease and less friction. For example, when mankind's relationship with God was intact, God brought the animals to mankind (the assignment) and man exercised his authority (governmental authority) to name whatever he encountered. Mankind's ability to properly identify God's creation correctly could only be accomplished with the leading and consultation of God. Without God, man's ability to exercise the authority released to him to lead and manage the Earth are given to error. This is where the unspoken and unrealized challenge appears. A prime example of man operating without God and the severe penalty it causes can be seen in the story of the Tower of Babel (Genesis 11:1-9). During this time mankind was unified in their plans and goals; they were on one accord and their vision and pursuit was void of God's inspiration, leading, instruction or inclusion. Their goal to touch heaven was aimless and served no purpose. As a result God visited them to assess their 'Godless' plans. This visitation caused God to acknowledge this important truth, *"Indeed* ***the people are one*** *and they all have one language, and this is what they begin to do;* ***now nothing that they propose to do will be withheld from them****"*. What this implies is when mankind is unified there is nothing within reason they cannot achieve. Their goals in building the Tower of Babel did not include God and in a unified effort they were engrossed in achieving something that did not align with His purpose in the Earth realm. As a result, God diversified their one language (tongue) into many, thus stopping or hindering their ability to communicate. In addition, God spread them out or grouped them together in the Earth according to their language (tongue).

Mankind's lawful and appropriate enjoyment of the Earth, the space created for him to be the governing authority was and is dependent upon our submission and obedience to the God. This requires each of us to make a choice to follow God way or reject God's way. All mankind had (and has) to do was choose to follow his Creator's instructions and remain submissively 'on one accord' with God. It is my theory that God, the Father created us to enjoy relationship and fellowship with us. I believe God created us to be 'hands on' with us. Why would God create mankind and the Earth with such attention to detail, to simply go off and not enjoy His creation? It is unfortunate that mankind's connection to God was disrupted and altered when Adam broke the connection due to his disobedience. In his disobedience which synonymous with going against the protective counsel of God, Adam cost all of mankind dearly. Let's examine the text:

Genesis 2:15-17

[15] *Then the LORD God took the man and put him in the Garden of Eden to tend and keep it.* [16] *And the LORD God* ***commanded the man (Adam)****, saying, "Of every tree of the garden you may freely eat;* [17] ***but of the tree of the knowledge of good and evil you shall not eat, for in the day that you eat of it you shall surely die.***"

This text now introduces the necessity of pleasing through obedience, which really translates into trust and faith. One of the definitions of "obey" in Webster's Dictionary is to be guided by. Synonyms of obey are follow, comply with, abide by and mind. What is the core of obedience? Obedience requires submission and submission requires trust. Thus I believe trust is at the core of obedience. For us to obey God and submit to His will and way, we must stay in a place of totaling trusting God and taking him at His Word in respect to positive and negative consequences. The following scripture supports this conclusion:

Proverbs 3:5-6

Trust in the LORD with all your heart, and lean not on your own understanding; [6] In all your ways acknowledge Him, and He shall direct your paths.

While there were many contributing variables revolving around how Satan strategically set Adam to fall, Adam's faith and trust in God wavered. There are many different theories of why it wavered. Was Adam blinded by God's love for him? Did Adam do it to protect Eve? Did Adam want to be like God as promised by Satan through Eve? Regardless of the reason you and I embrace personally, we would do well to recognize that Adam missed the full magnitude or importance of trusting God to be a God of His

Word above all. God was so mindful of Adam, giving to Adam, so kind to Adam, such a friend to Adam, that Adam may have grossly underestimated God's dedication to His Word. God's dedication to His Word supersedes His love for an individual, it locks His intervention. Adam did not have the advantage of having the Bible to learn that once God decrees or gives His word on a matter He will not go against, even though he can. God's love for Adam would not deter or cause God to omit delivering on what he promised. Sidebar: The same goes for you and me. I believe we allow the greatness of God's love for us to create a false narrative, for God will not go against His Word. **We must shift our mindsets to see God's instruction as a protective agent and not a limiting restriction**. What good thing would a loving father withhold from his child? What loving father would not try to protect his child from harm? Let's examine all the mistakes we made, having full knowledge of how God operates. Do you think we should cut Adam a break, after examining ourselves?

2.7: GOD'S RELATIONAL INTENT

I would like to the opportunity to validate my theory regarding God's intent to enjoy a personal and physical 'hands on' relationship with mankind, using Genesis 3:8. In the scripture God the Father, the Creator came to enjoy, visit and communicate with man (His creation). It is my theory that God the Father was physically present, walking in Eden. Having said this, it can be deduced that I do not subscribe to the Christophany Theory as many that I respect and honor do. The Christophany theory contends that every time God the Father visited Earth in physical form, He came as pre-incarnate Christ. I believe the Christophany theory is man's attempt to try to explain an aspect of God's being, composition or movement that cannot be concretely be explained by man due to our limited perspective. I do not believe we should definitively attempt to explain God's movement by using man made concepts. I believe this puts limits on a limitless God. Please remember that before Adam ate off the forbidden Tree of the Knowledge of Good and Evil, sin was not a part of his composition. After Adam disobeyed God, his composition and fabric was altered and thus mankind's ability to be in the presence of a Holy God wrapped in sinful flesh was affected.

On day seven God rested and beheld His creation completed and He blessed the day and decided it was to be a day dedicated unto the Lord, a day of rest or reset. He then comes back to communicate and be among what He had created. God desired (purposed) to enjoy the fellowship and interaction with man (His creation). Let's examine the text.

Genesis3:8

And they ***heard the sound of the Lord God walking*** *in the garden in the cool of the day, and* ***Adam and his wife hid themselves from the presence of the Lord God*** *among the trees of the garden.* [9] *Then the LORD God called to Adam and said to him, "Where are you?"* [10] *So he said, "I heard Your voice in the garden, and I was afraid because I was naked; and* ***I hid myself****."* [11] *And He said, "Who told you that you were naked? Have you eaten from the tree of which I commanded you that you should not eat?"* [12] *Then the man said, "The woman whom You gave to be with me, she gave me of the tree, and I ate."* [13] *And the LORD God said to the woman, "What is this you have done?"*

From the text we deduce God's visiting Adam to fellowship with His creation was a normal occurrence. Adam's sin caused him to hide from God's physical presence, it caused him to be spiritually out of position to encounter God in the manner he enjoyed previously.

Let's go to another passage of scripture and let us arm ourselves with the knowledge that God plans from the end of a thing to the beginning. This allows me to understand that God decides the conclusion of a matter or its purpose and plans accordingly. Considering this, let's examine the Book of Revelation to further support God's intent or desire to be hands on with man.

Revelation 21:3-7 and 22:2-4

And I heard a loud voice from heaven saying, "Behold, ***the tabernacle of God is with men****, and* ***He will dwell with them****, and they shall be His people.* ***God Himself will be with them*** *and be their God. [4] And God will wipe away every tear from their eyes; there shall be no more death, nor sorrow, nor crying. There shall be no more pain, for the former things have passed away." [5] Then He who sat on the throne said, "Behold, I make all things new." And He said to me, "Write, for these words are true and faithful." [6] And He said to me, "It is done! I am the Alpha and the Omega, the Beginning and the End. I will give of the fountain of the water of life freely to him who thirsts. [7] He who overcomes shall inherit all things, and I will be his God and he shall be My son.*

Revelation 22:2-4

In the middle of its street, and on either side of the river, was the tree of life, which bore twelve fruits, each tree yielding its fruit every month. The leaves of the tree were for the healing of the nations. [3] *And there shall be no more curse,* ***but the throne of God (the Father, the Creator) and of the Lamb (Jesus Christ the Son) shall be in it****, and His servants shall serve Him.* [4] ***They shall see His face****, and His name shall be on their foreheads.*

Previously I asked the question, "Why does a Creator construct something unless it is the intent to enjoy or take advantage of it in some way or benefit from the thing produced?" In the classic story book Geppetto (the creator) created Pinocchio with the intent of enjoying fellowship and interaction with Pinocchio. Geppetto enjoyed Pinocchio's company immensely until Pinocchio did not heed Geppetto's protective instruction and pursued his own agenda which took him on a road of 'clear and present danger'. Deceivingly, this road to destruction was presented to Pinocchio as a road that would be full of unending and unlimited good times. This road however caused Pinocchio to become a prisoner and pawn to profit someone else's agenda. In the absence of Pinocchio, Geppetto was greatly saddened because he was separated from his creation. However, when Pinocchio found his way home Geppetto was overjoyed.

Without the guidance of Geppetto, Pinocchio continuously fell prey to an agenda beyond his comprehension. He really was ignorant of the demonic and wicked forces that existed outside of Geppetto's covering, forces that wanted to capitalize on what Pinocchio uniquely had to offer for their own profit and to bring about his demise.

The fictional character Geppetto fashions the intent of our non-fiction God and Pinocchio that of man. God wanted to have a relationship with Adam; He wants to have a relationship you and me. In addition, God wants to guide us as we complete the purpose He assigned. This may help explain why God did something uniquely different in creating man. He breathed into the nostrils of man and then man became a living creature (Genesis 2:7). Man having the nature, quality or likeness of God is something all the other things created on Earth prior lacked, God's Spirit (Genesis 1:26). But it did not stop there. Instructions and dominion were entrusted and given to man over all the creation on Earth that preceded him (Genesis 1:27-30). God wanted man to somewhat mimic and represent His authority here in the Earth realm.

When Adam sinned it changed the course of how mankind would exist on Earth, the pure unrestricted relationship between God and man, and how man perceived things.

Today, it is vital that those submitted to God, **pursue influencing our culture and guiding civilization daily**. Ambassadors for the Kingdom of God have the ability to influence our culture and guide our civilization by using the gifts released to us in the fashion God intended. Key variables in the proper use of our gifts to influence the Earth realm is timing and placement.

When men and women are submitted to God, we are stronger, better advised and protected. Thomas Aquinas said, "The best way to attain goodness is to abandon worldly things and seek communion with God". Satan endeavors to sow seeds of discord between the Creator and His creation, in hopes of **disrupting communication and to hinder unity**. When believers are out of proper relationship with God, it causes us to be 'out of sync' with His agenda, thus leaving the Earth vulnerable to the deception of Satan. This opens us up to being vessels of dishonor and not receiving 'the spoils' or reward of being in unity with God's agenda. Let's examine the following text to see how one wrong decision can affect our lives:

Genesis 3:17-19; 22-24

*[17] Then to Adam He said, "Because you have heeded the voice of your wife, and have eaten from the tree of which I commanded you, saying, 'You shall not eat of it': "***Cursed is the ground for your sake; in toil you shall eat of it all the days of your life.** *[18] Both thorns and thistles it shall bring forth for you, and you shall eat the herb of the field.* ***[19] In the sweat of your face you shall eat bread till you return to the ground, for out of it you were taken; for dust you are, and to dust you shall return.***" *[22] Then the LORD God said, "Behold, the man has become like one of Us, to know good and evil. And now, lest he put out his hand and take also of the tree of life, and eat, and live forever" – [23] therefore the LORD God sent him out of the garden of Eden to till the ground from which he was taken. [24] So He drove out the man; and He placed cherubim at the east of the Garden of Eden, and a flaming sword which turned every way, to guard the way to the tree of life.*

Genesis 6:3

*And the Lord said, "***My Spirit shall not strive with man forever***, for he is indeed flesh; yet his days shall be one hundred and twenty years."*

As we progress in text from Genesis to Exodus, we see over time the interaction with God in man became more significantly altered as time progressed. For example, there is a distinct difference in how God interacted with Adam vs. how he interacted with Moses. Moses was hid in the clef of the rock to protect him from dying from being in God's presence due to the DNA of sin in his flesh, transferred from Adam. Let's look to the text:

Exodus 33:20-23

[20] *But He (God) said, "**You cannot see My face; for no man shall see Me, and live.**" [21] And the LORD said, "Here is a place by Me, and you shall stand on the rock. [22] So it shall be, while My glory passes by, that I will put you in the cleft of the rock, and will cover you with My hand while I pass by. [23] Then I will take away My hand, and you shall see My back; but My face shall not be seen."*

The effects of Adam sin were major and definitely beyond Adam's comprehension and highly consequential for all of his seed including you and me. Our mindset separated from God's leading and consultation only becomes exceedingly wicked. We see evidence of this in the introduction of the story of Noah and then in Noah's descendant's after God cleansed the Earth in the story of the Tower of Babel:

Genesis 6:5

Then the Lord saw that ***the wickedness of man was great*** *in the earth, and that* ***every intent of the thoughts of his heart was only evil continually****. [6] And the Lord was sorry that He had made man on the earth, and He was grieved in His heart. [7] So the Lord said, "I will destroy man whom I have created from the face of the earth, both man and beast, creeping thing and birds of the air, for I am sorry that I have made them." [8] But Noah found grace in the eyes of the Lord. [9] This is the genealogy of Noah. Noah was a just man, perfect in his generations. Noah walked with God. [10] And Noah begot three sons: Shem, Ham, and Japheth. [11]* ***The earth also was corrupt before God, and the earth was filled with violence.*** *[12] So God looked upon the earth, and indeed it was corrupt; for* ***all flesh had corrupted their way on the earth****.*

Genesis 11: 1, 4-9

Now the whole earth had one language and one speech. [4] And they said, "Come, let us ***build ourselves a city****, and a tower whose top is in the heavens; let* ***us make a name for ourselves****, lest we be scattered abroad over the face of the whole earth." [5] But the Lord came down to see the city and the tower which the sons of men had built. [6] And the Lord said, "Indeed the people are one and they all have one language, and this is what they begin to do; now nothing that they propose to do will be withheld from them. [7] Come, let Us go down and there confuse their language (DCS – unified effort), that they may not understand one another's speech." [8] So the Lord* *scattered them abroad from there over the face of all the earth, and they ceased building the city.* [9] *Therefore its name is called Babel, because there the Lord confused the language of all the earth; and from there the Lord scattered them abroad over the face of all the earth.*

For us to completely understand what we are to do, how we are to do it, and to what end, we must get this information from the mind of the Creator. For us to know how to best utilize what is provided for us, we must seek the mind of the Creator.

Because our hearts are deceitfully wicked, we cannot trust what always comes out of it. The word of God also lets us know that in our flesh dwells no good thing. The word of God also advises us the wide is the way that leads to death and destruction but narrow is the way the leads to life and there are few that find it. We cannot trust ourselves, we must be dependent on our constant connection to God to be led to what is true and what is best. King Solomon, one of the wisest men of his time emphasizes this in two passages of scripture—the same warning and advice:

Proverbs 14:12; 16:25 –
There is a way which seemeth right unto a man, but the end thereof are the ways of death.

To add another layer of understanding to this, speaking through the Prophet Isaiah God shared this:

Isaiah 55:8-11

"For My thoughts are not your thoughts, nor are your ways My ways," says the Lord. [9] "For as the heavens are higher than the earth, so are My ways higher than your ways, And My thoughts than your thoughts". [10] For as the rain comes down, and the snow from heaven, and do not return there, but water the earth, And make it bring forth and bud, That it may give seed to the sower and bread to the eater, [11] So shall My word be that goes forth from My mouth; It shall not return to Me [c]void, But it shall accomplish what I please, and it shall prosper in the thing for which I sent it.

Paul taught the church of Corinth the following:

I Corinthians 1:27-29

But God has chosen the foolish things of the world to put to shame the wise, and God has chosen the weak things of the world to put to shame the things which are mighty; [28] and the base things of the world and the things which are despised God has chosen, and the things which are not, to bring to nothing the things that are, [29] that no flesh should glory in His presence.

The proper position to have when trying to gain knowledge and understanding of God is that of a child, an infant. We must never lose sight that we exist by the will of God the Creator. Through ups and downs, trials and tribulations, good times and bad, we must not forget that we have a Creator that pre-determined, or pre-planned certain things to be. God's pre-determinations are also referred to as God's **perfect will**. Knowing and understanding the perfect will of God helps us to be in alignment with (and not in violation of) God's **permissive will**.

The permissive will of God is where our freedom lies. If the perfect will dictates where we must go; what we must do in certain instances; predetermines 'the Who', what, when and why—then our only option within the perfect will is to decide or choose the how. In God's permissive will 'the Who', what, when and why are left in our hands. Correspondingly, we show our spiritual maturity and allegiance to God in the realm of God's permissive will and the how (as a vessel of honor or dishonor) within context of His perfect will. Our heart's desire should be the decisions we make in God's permissive will to be in alignment with or run completely parallel to God's perfect will. Let's use the following graph to explain:

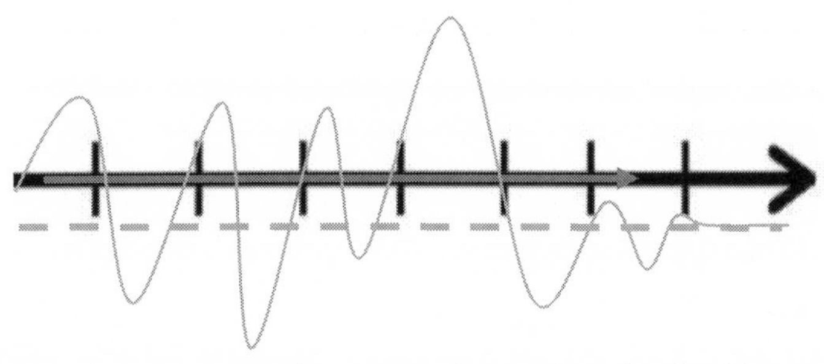

Often it is advised that straight path is both always the best and the fastest. While this may be up for debate depending on the variables in specific situations, it is absolutely factual pertaining to the path we take to pleasing God or being in alignment with Him. In the graph above the thick horizontal black line represents the perfect will of God and the vertical black lines represent things we must do, things that must happen and things that must be. These vertical black lines plotted along the way are preordained occurrences throughout time that God predetermined we must experience as we precede forward in life. These preordained occurrences or intersections vary in nature; they could be people, places, things, situations, etc. Some of the predetermined intersections are put in place for us to be influenced, for us to influence or a combination of the both. Do you remember the movie 'Back to the Future'? In the movie, Michael J. Fox traveled though time and quickly learned that his mere presence, in even the most minimal way had the ability to influence the past and thus change the outcome in the future. From this movie, we see a display of how things are influenced beyond our comprehension or realization. Remember, based on the way God operates we may or may not ever learn why God preordained these vertical line occurrences or predetermined something to be.

The grey 'curvy' line represents the decisions or steps of someone who does not consider the predetermined purpose or predetermined of God. Unfortunately, throughout the life of this individual, invaluable time is wasted, as they spend a great amount of time traveling away from what God has willed to be, only to have to travel back to intersect with those predetermined points (vertical short black lines). If we follow this wayward path, time is wasted and we sign up for collisions designed to redirect us and align us with what the will of God dictates must be.

The grey dotted line represents the decisions of someone who considers, respects and submits to God's perfect will or pre-determined plan. Their steps are parallel to what God has purposed to be, they do not conflict, oppose or challenge what God's predetermined purpose dictates. This path welcomes and invites the favor of God to work on their behalf. This path is not void of test and trials, but those encountered are minimal in comparison to the one traveling giving no thought to God. This truth should make these scriptures become more significant in our lives: makes the following scriptures 'hit' or affect us differently.

Psalms 37:23

The steps of God man are ordered by the Lord, and He delights in his way.

Proverbs 3:6

Acknowledge Him in all thy ways and He shall will direct your paths.

The key to having a successful and abundant life is seeking God to learn what His perfect will is. After we are armed with this information, then and only then are we able to be positioned not to violate or go against God's perfect will in the realm of His permissive will. Hopefully, this information has caused you to consider the gravity of your decisions and the importance of being submitted to God's will. The following questions should always proceed our movement, **"God what are you up to?" and "God what do you expect of me?"** Since we are asking questions, let's ask other important questions: Is it my responsibility to find out what God is up to and my role within it? Can what I don't know hurt me? Let's explore these scriptures to assist us in answering these questions:

- Solomon suggests that getting an understanding is crucial for progression in life (Proverbs 4:7).
- The Apostle Paul advises his apprentice Timothy to study the Word of God so that he would be a follower that has no need to be ashamed, but rather is approved (II Timothy 2:15).
- The Psalmist highlights that the Word of God is as a lamp unto our feet and a light for our path (Psalms 119:105).
- God used the prophet Hosea to place His followers on high alert in understanding that God's own perish directly due to a lack of knowledge (Hosea 4:6).

According to the Bible, God has a definite plan and order. Many live life oblivious to the fact that there is a plan and order of God. In God's unmerited love for us and His infinite wisdom, he constructed a user guide to lead us to learn Him and reveal His overarching plan, which we refer to as the Bible. I can testify about the importance of having a user guide from personal experience.

I have two experiences I would like to share. My wife and I have had a few vehicles. Each vehicle had some similarities in how they functioned and ignorantly I relied on information I learned from a previous vehicle to help me diagnose and address the problems that arose another. Not referring to the manual could have caused significant damage or eventually ruined the vehicle I depended on to transport not only myself, but more importantly my family, to future destinations.

The first example revolves around the type of gas needed to fuel the vehicle (low, middle, or premium grade gas) and the type of oil needed (standard or synthetic, 5W-20 or 10W-40). Both the gas and the motor oil are vital to proper functioning and forward movement of the vehicle. The gas provides the needed substance to turn the vehicle on and allow forward momentum. A previous car did not call for using the best grade of gas, there was no specification. In addition, I had heard countless conversations suggesting that the grade of gas used affecting the performance of a vehicle to be only be a myth. To save money I ignored the advisory message on the gas cap and used low-grade gas to be more economical. When I stepped on the gas pedal to accelerate I noticed an immediate difference in the performance of the car. The difference was so noticeable that it caused me to be concerned over time. This led me to read the manual about the car's performance. After reading the manual, I came to understand that the grade of gas used in the vehicle immediately affects the performance of the cars acceleration and over the course of time deposits left by using more economical grades could cause major damage and jeopardize the life expectancy of the vehicle.

The second example involved the type engine oil needed to provide lubrication to the metal parts working internally in the engine. These metal components, together with minimal friction, were needed to insure a smooth performance. Growing up my father usually had 8 cylinder Cadillac cars. My father taught me the basics of car maintenance early and this included knowing how to fill all the fluids in a car. Older 8 cylinder Cadillac's called for using 10W-40 oil. I had no idea what the true difference was between 10W-40, 5W-30, or 0W-20. I just knew that Cadillacs were luxury cars, so I assumed if it was good enough for a Cadillac it was the best for any other car. Let's fast forward. My brother's first car was a 4 cylinder 1984 Chevy Celebrity. In his young adult years my brother had no clue about the engine of car and fluid maintenance. When my brother asked what type of oil my father's car used I told him 10W-40. He then proceeded to put 10W-40 meant for an 8 cylinder car in a 4 cylinder car. Over a short amount of time the cars performance was out of sync and my brother had no idea why. After reading the manual, I learned my brothers 4 cylinder Chevy Celebrity called for using the 5W-20. After reading the manual and asking around I discovered the differences between the oil types was in the primarily in the thickness of the oil. 10W-40 oil was too thick for my brothers 4 cylinder car and overtime could have caused major damage and hindered performance. From this, I quickly learned that making an innocent mistake due to pure ignorance or assumption can cause the vehicle I depended upon to malfunction, thus hindering proper or normal operation and threatening the vehicle's life expectancy.

From these problems I gained a whole new appreciation for manufacturers that provide manuals to guide consumers in the use their product—especially those with detailed descriptions, explanations and instructions. I purchased a used car that had no manual in it. When my wife had a problem with the car, I looked for the manual in the glove compartment, but it was not there. I then looked under the seats and in the trunk; it was not there either. I then asked my wife, "where is the manual for the car?" She responded, "It didn't come with one." The previous owners did not leave the manual in the car, and the car lot she purchased it from had not replaced it. Suddenly, I recognized my journey to gain knowledge and understanding about the vehicle would be halted unless I accessed the manual. Without the manual, I lacked the ability to address the problem that had risen and evaluate the symptoms. A warning light appeared on the dashboard, but I needed the manual to understand the nature and purpose of the warning. It could have meant the vehicle was in immediate danger or that while it was not in immediate danger, continued use in the current condition could cause major harm. A choice was before me, I could remain frustrated and proceed operating the vehicle in ignorance, unaware of what type of damage continued use would cause, or I could take the car to the station. Here's where my appreciation for trained technicians grew.

It was not a good feeling to have to visit a repair station and allow a technician to evaluate it due to my being incapable of arriving at an answer on my own. However, wisdom dictated that I submit to the knowledge of one trained to gain understanding regarding the caution lights and associated minor symptoms of malfunctioning. I chose to humble myself and submit to one who had knowledge and understanding I did not possess. At the service station, a trained technician with experience in addressing issues surrounding the vehicle could aid me in the fixing problem. This experience allowed me to have great appreciation for technicians trained to aid me in addressing issues when they emerge.

If a human manufacturer or creator wants the patron, receiver, or purchaser of their product to be able to maximize the use of their creation, what about God? Would God want us to go through life with no manual or guide? How then would we learn of Him? How would we be in alignment to live according to the purpose He predetermined? God, our Creator was indeed thoughtful enough to provide us with a manual, a way to access His mind, a book of testimony. We refer to it as the Bible. The Bible gives insight and instruction on:

1. The relationship between God and mankind corporately,
2. Our personal individual relationship to God,
3. How to access Him, and
4. How to proceed through life in harmony with Him.

These four things are just the beginning of the advantages of reading knowing, understanding and adhering to the Bible as we live life. II Timothy 3 and James 1 reveal powerful truth about the origin and purpose of the Bible and the importance of our mindset in pursuit of unlocking its truths.

<u>II Timothy 3:16-17</u>

All scripture is given by inspiration of God, and is profitable for doctrine, for reproof, for correction, for instruction in righteousness. [17] That the man of God may be complete, thoroughly equipped for every good work.

James 1:5-8

[5] *If any of you lacks wisdom, let him ask of God, who gives to all liberally and without reproach, and it will be given to him.* [6] ***But let him ask in faith, with no doubting, for he who doubts is like a wave of the sea driven and tossed by the wind.*** [7] ***For let not that man suppose that he will receive anything from the Lord;*** [8] ***he is a double-minded man, unstable in all his ways.***

These scriptures allow us to understand God wants to reveal Himself to anyone who has a sincere desire to know Him. However, full disclosure of His truth is not revealed to all. Our motive for seeking God is paramount in Him choosing to reveal Himself to you. In simple terms if you are seeking to disprove God's existence, authority, or word your motive is not pure, and you will not be granted the illumination needed to understand beyond the words written. If you desire to learn of God for purposes of selfish gain, or misuse of application, your motive is not pure. Please do not presume you will be granted the illumination needed to understand beyond the literal words. Learning God requires a position of submission. I have learned partial submission does not pave the way to full disclosure. In Psalms 24, a question is asked regarding who can ascend into the place where God dwells. The answer given paraphrased was he who has clean hands, a pure heart, not given to idols and who is not deceitful.

To gain a better understanding of God the Creator, our heavenly Father, we must utilize the manual or guide He provided the Bible, His Word. To those who seek to discard the Bible and do not accept it as the Word of God because it was delivered by man, I ask the following question. Isn't the majority of all we believe and hold true, dealing with history and even the recollection of present occurrences mostly dependent upon testimony?' In the court of law, isn't the testimony of one credible witness enough to send a person to jail? Before the age of recording devices by way of audio and visuals we only had testimony. Why believe in a God that would not provide a manual or a guide for His creation to follow? If we wanted to prove the validity of a testimony, would we not gather experts and the best minds—trusted and proven individuals from among our society—to develop ways to authenticate the truth of the testimony offered?

I believe fully understanding God's purpose for Earth and mankind is dependent upon learning the Bible, the Word of God given to guide us. After we acquire knowledge and arrive at a position understanding, we must ask God the Father (the Creator) to give us wisdom to properly apply the knowledge and understanding we have attained.

Studying God's Word, the Bible, not only unlocks our ability to gain knowledge and understand God our Creator, it also gives us insight to into what He has created, how to live within His creation and how to live as His creation. One's interpretation of God and His creations are extremely limited without knowing the Bible. As previously mentioned, one can experience God or be used by God and yet not know God. Let's qualify this through this fictional story, a Pastor Stewart parable.

Imagine you have been confined in a room without windows from birth until the age of eighteen. Out of nowhere Mr. Witness comes along to free you. He tells you that you had the potential to gain freedom by simply taking the time to read and learn from a book that has been in desk by your bed for 18 years. He further notifies you that he is only able to grant you temporary freedom and that you must wear a blindfold. You, eager to just get out, ignorantly choose not gain permanent freedom by reading and learning the book because you rather depend on Mr. Witness. Mr. Witness agrees to help you, reiterating the condition that you must be blindfolded the entire time you were out of the room until you return.

Blindfolded you are guided by Mr. Witness to a vehicle. Riding along you begin to <u>feel</u> the wind brush against your hair and you <u>hear</u> a host of different sounds; however, you cannot see to identify you are in a convertible. You arrive at a restaurant, you do not know the name or type of restaurant, all you know is you <u>smell</u> different aromas. Mr. Witness orders for you without consulting you. Mr. Witness says open wide, bite down and chew and you heed his command. The <u>taste</u> of the food starts exploding in your mouth. After consuming your food you, having experienced a series of new and exciting things while being blindfolded, are guided back to your confined room and the door is shut.

Due to you being blindfolded you experienced new sounds, feelings, smells and taste however you have no idea what you experienced, or how to get back them on your own. You are dependent on Mr. Witness to come get you and guide you to the same thing and beyond. Your mind begins to think, "What else is out there to experience?" Frustration really begins to kick in because you are now mentally reminiscing on all the new things experienced, and you are now imagining more. You now consider reading the book, merely glanced at all of your life, because you remember Mr. Witness advising you that your freedom is in your hands, but only to be attained by reading the book for yourself.

Once you begin reading it, you are able to get out; however, you have no idea the type of vehicle you rode in, what restaurant you ate in or what food you ate. Your ability to return for a new experience is hindered because you choose to be blindfolded and guided by someone else. This fictional story is what is like for someone who does not believe in and read the Word of God.

This is how most people live life in general. We gravitate to what is fastest even if it sacrifices what is best, more profitable long term, or puts at risk what is best. Let's look at cooking habits for example. We use the microwave over the stove because it gets us our food faster, totally ignoring the health warnings regarding it not being healthy. In vegetable preparation, how many of us reach for the can, bagged frozen vegetables or pre-chopped vegetables, rather than going to the farmers market to get fresh vegetables that have to be cleaned and prepared by us, because we know the dangers associated with can goods and bagged vegetables. Another example can be seen in how we assemble something. How many of us have brought something that required assembly and chose to look at the picture of the product on the box, skim over the directions and proceed to assemble the product? At the end we usually say "Hmmm, what are these for? Oh well it will be alright". Most of us will never choose the road that requires more time or greater discipline. We opt to reach our desired end as quickly as possible, and promise ourselves that we will take the time needed to have a better experience next time.

Unfortunately, many handle God the same way. Rather than taking the time to read and learn about Him for ourselves, we settle for functioning off of the knowledge, understanding or experience of another. Instead of securing our own connection to Him, we settle for a third party experience through another. To put it bluntly, a budding, maturing and progressive relationship with God at times just hasn't been worth our time. We want the benefits of God without having a relationship with God. Simply put, we want God on our terms and we desire His involvement in our lives based on our determined timelines. We don't' want to take the time needed, nor do we want to live according to the prescribed, disciplined format. This approach to living leaves a void and guarantees we operate with deficit. A mature adult understands any healthy relationship takes times to develop, needs consistent communication and comes with boundaries, limitations and acceptances.

God desires to have a personal relationship with each of us. He has paved the way for such an opportunity to be possible. How fantastic is it that God wants us to know His plan, His preferences and His judgment regarding matters we encounter as we live life daily.

God has given us a tool to position us properly as we endeavor to learn Him, know Him, be in agreement by Him, be used by Him, etc. The tool is the Bible. Without the Bible, I believe our spiritual development is severely crippled. The Bible's divinely inspired content empowers us to learn God's character, His plan, His truth and His protective directions and instructions. Like those who did not have the Bible, we would learn through our experience on some levels, but the Bible enables us to examine our experiences through God's lens. The faithfulness of God unto man is indescribable! He allows us to see things as He sees them, to interpret and examine with Godly perspective. The reality is God can use us in phenomenal ways. Though we are clueless, He invites us to partner with Him. The opportunity for us to know and understand God on *authorized levels* is available to us; however, we must choose to seize it. Refusing to utilize the Bible assures one will never establish or position oneself to enjoy a progressive and maturing relationship with our Creator, the relationship that will grant us access to knowing and respecting what He has created and allowed to be. Without the Bible we cannot properly trace our steps with accuracy;, we're confined like the man in the room, blinded.

CHAPTER 3

God, the Son

3.1: THE WHY
Identifying the Need

Understanding God's plans from the end to the beginning is extremely beneficial and gives us great insight into the strategy God enlisted as He deliberately created. It also helps us understand that God did not wait until man sinned to create a plan to redeem him to be repositioned back into alignment with His purpose. God had a plan of redemption established before he formed Adam from the dust of the Earth. Knowing His purpose, He made a means to assure it would be protected.

Man was not God the Father's first creation in the universe or on Earth. God witnessed the error of creations that preceded us, which armed Him with the probability of mankind falling prey to the deception of Satan. If Satan, the Fallen Archangel Lucifer was able to persuade a third of all of heaven to depart and follow Him, surely God knew mankind having 'free-will' within His 'perfect-will', made Him a prime target for Satan and how mankind faltering would endanger their position within His plan. Again, because God planned from the end to the beginning, he always sets things up to secure His purpose is fulfilled without fail. Based on this, it is safe to suggest that in His infinite wisdom, God had a plan to save or redeem mankind, in the event we should fall. God created us as agents with a measure of 'free-will' or choice (His permissive will), so God had a plan of salvation built in from the beginning. If Satan Lucifer was able to persuade one-third of angels or heavenly beings to rebel against God, causing them to be banished (evicted) from heaven to Earth, it was probable that Lucifer and his cohorts may try to influence God's authorized ruling authority in the Earth realm, His latest creation, mankind.

Mankind had a conditional eternal covenant with God that was based upon Adam adhering to the instruction given to keep the covenant intact. Satan, being a former archangel, has 'first-hand' knowledge and experience regarding the systems of God and His Kingdom. Thus, Satan knew his only way of getting man to disrupt His connection with God and allow him to become his prey, would be to cause mankind (Adam) to break covenant. Unfortunately, Adam did fall for Satan's clever trap and altered his existence and the state for all of mankind following him; as he would be the progenitor (i.e., the originator). For believers living on the other side of Adam's fall, we understand the most severe consequence of Adam's breaking covenant, through disobedience (sin) includes the alteration of our perception, our spiritual connection to God and disrupted physical fellowship with God. To keep the covenant intact, Adam only needed to trust the Word (warning) of God and obey God's instruction not to eat from one tree, the Tree of the Knowledge of God and Evil.

Once Adam ate of the Tree of the Knowledge of Good and Evil, God's plan of salvation to redeem mankind came 'online' or went into effect. Based on God granting mankind governmental authority within the Earth, a man was needed to rectify or pardon the damage caused by Adam. Romans chapter 5, indicates by one man (Adam), all of mankind was sentenced and by another man (Jesus Christ) they would have the opportunity to be redeemed. God created a type of second Adam in bringing forth Jesus Christ, a man not from the seed of Adam, one worthy of redeeming mankind from the penalty of Adam's sin, a man who would be an acceptable sacrifice. The release of mankind from the penalty of spiritual death, being disconnected from their Creator eternally and living life under the bondage of sin would ride on the spiritual fortitude of this man. Romans the 5th chapter gives a detailed explanation of the condemnation that resulted from Adam's sin and the redemption made available through Jesus Christ.

<u>Romans 5:12-21</u>

[12] Therefore, just as through one man sin entered the world, and death through sin, and thus death spread to all men, because all sinned – [13] (For until the law sin was in the world, but sin is not imputed when there is no law. [14] Nevertheless death reigned from Adam to Moses, even over those who had not sinned according to the likeness of the transgression of Adam, who is a type of Him who was to come. [15] But the free gift is not like the offense. For if by the one man's offense many died, much more the grace of God and the gift by the grace of the one Man, Jesus Christ, abounded to many. [16] And the gift is not like that which came through the one who sinned. For the judgment which came from one offense resulted in condemnation, but the free gift which came from many [b]offenses resulted in justification. [17] For if by the one man's [c]offense death reigned through the one, much more those who receive abundance of grace and of the gift of righteousness will reign in life through the One, Jesus Christ.) [18] Therefore, as through one man's offense judgment came to all men, resulting in condemnation, even so through one Man's

righteous act the free gift came to all men, resulting in justification of life. [19] For as by one man's disobedience many were made sinners, so also by one Man's obedience many will be made righteous. [20] Moreover the law entered that the offense might abound. But where sin abounded, grace abounded much more, [21] so that as sin reigned in death, even so grace might reign through righteousness to eternal life through Jesus Christ our Lord.

Let's take a look at these scriptures to help us understand the power that belief in Christ makes available in the life of those who believe.

John 4:14

[14] but whoever drinks of the water that I shall give him will never thirst. But the water that I shall give him will become in him a fountain of water springing up into everlasting life."

John 3:34

[34] For He whom God has sent speaks the words of God, for God does not give the Spirit by measure.

John 5:26-30

[26] For as the Father has life in Himself, so He has granted the Son to have life in Himself, [27] and has given Him authority to execute judgment also, because He is the Son of Man. [28] Do not marvel at this; for the hour is coming in which all who are in the graves

will hear His voice [29] and come forth – those who have done good, to the resurrection of life, and those who have done evil, to the resurrection of condemnation. [30] I can of Myself do nothing. As I hear, I judge; and My judgment is righteous, because I do not seek My own will but the will of the Father who sent Me.

John 14:6

[6] Jesus said to him, "I am the way, the truth, and the life. No one comes to the Father except through Me.

Adam's sin initiated the need of God's insurance plan for man, Jesus Christ to go into effect. These scriptures allow us to understand the redemptive, life-altering power of belief in Jesus Christ. Hopefully, reading this section has helped you understand the need mankind has for the redemptive work of Christ.

3.2: THE HOW.

This section is designed to explain through scripture, how God manifested or caused our Redeemer, Jesus Christ to be. The truths or facts surrounding the conception of Jesus Christ, is where I believe man must really exercise caution and not question why God would do it this way, as to assess whether God's chosen method makes 'human sense' We must be careful not question God from a position of disrespect, judgement, or doubt. We must remember His ways and thoughts are not like ours and that He chooses the foolish things of the world to confound the wise. This is where trusting God is 'God enough' to materialize the best plan according to what He has created and purposed to be comes into play. In the previous section 'The Need. The Why', Romans chapter 5, helped us establish a solid foundation of the need of the redemptive work of Jesus Christ. Now we will examine the scriptures to examine or layout 'The How' regarding the conception of Jesus Christ.

Please allow me to give this brief 'overview' before we examine the text. We understand all of Adam's seed inherits the DNA of sin. Hence, none of Adam's seed (man born of the seed of man) would be an acceptable deliverer, due to the sin nature within that renders us, an impure or unacceptable sacrifice. Let's think back to the Old Testament and God's attention to detail regarding sacrifices and the requirement that certain sacrifices be without blemish. Based upon this, God would have to come up with a way to impregnate a woman free from the seed of sinful man, to serve as an acceptable sacrifice or 'repairer of the breach'.

God, in His infinite wisdom impregnated a virgin named Mary, the mother of Jesus with the very Word of God. Please remember everything created in Genesis, was manifested by God speaking (His Word) it into existence. This allowed Christ to qualify as an acceptable sacrifice without the DNA of sin. Believing in the complete story of Christ positions us to confess our faith, trust and submission to God the Father. Faith, in God's plan of redemption through Christ is the only way to receive salvation (to be pardoned from the penalty of sin) and for the connection to be fully restored with God the Father. Let us look at the following scriptures to confirm.

<u>John 1:14</u>

[14] ***And the Word was made flesh, and dwelt among us,*** *(and we beheld His glory, the glory as of the only begotten of the Father,) full of grace and truth.*

<u>John 3:16-18</u>

[16] ***For God so loved the world that He gave His only begotten Son, that whoever believes in Him should not perish but have everlasting life.*** [17] *For God did not send His Son into the world to condemn the world, but that the world through Him might be saved.* [18] *"He who believes in Him is not condemned; but he who does not believe is condemned already, because he has not believed in the name of the only begotten Son of God.*

<u>Matthew 1:18-23</u>

[18] *Now the birth of Jesus Christ was as follows: After His mother Mary was betrothed to Joseph, before they came together, she was found with child of the Holy Spirit.* [19] *Then Joseph her husband, being a just man, and not wanting to make her a public example, was minded to put her away secretly.* [20] *But while he thought about these things, behold, an angel of the Lord appeared to him in a dream, saying, "Joseph, son of David, do not be afraid to take to you Mary your wife, for that which is conceived in her is of the Holy Spirit.* [21] ***And she will bring forth a Son, and you shall call His name JESUS, for He will save His people from their sins."*** [22] *So all this was done that it might be fulfilled which was*

spoken by the Lord through the prophet, saying: [23] *"Behold, the virgin shall be with child, and bear a Son, and they shall call His name Immanuel," which is translated, "God with us."*

<u>John 3:33-35</u>

[33] ***He who has received His testimony has certified that God is true.*** [34] *For He whom God has sent speaks the words of God, for God does not give the Spirit by measure.* [35] ***The Father loves the Son, and has given all things into His hand.***

<u>John 14:6</u>

[6] ***Jesus said to him, "I am the way, the truth, and the life. No one comes to the Father except through Me.***

Based on these passages of scripture we see how God chose to bring about Jesus Christ, our redeemer. In addition, we learn how one accepts and walks in the salvation made available through belief in Jesus Christ (Word of God made flesh into a seed, implanted into Mary).

3.3: THE REASON

Part I

Christ Foundational Identity & Correlating Function

To really unlock the power of Jesus Christ in the Trinity, I believe it is crucial to really grasp that He is literally the Word of God made flesh. Jesus Christ is referenced to have been with God since the beginning per John 1:1-5. Based upon this scripture, Christ's true existence pre-dates His arrival as Jesus Christ in the flesh. Jesus Christ says, "Whatever you ask in my name" or "Whatever you ask based on my identity (purposed function) will be granted unto you". To add a layer and get proper perspective James teaches and cautions us to be certain not to ask amiss or not in accordance with the Word of God over our lives individually and corporately. Acceptance of Jesus Christ is acceptance of the Word and denial of Jesus Christ is denial of the complete Word of God. This helps understand why Jesus Christ stated, "I am the way, the truth and the life. No one comes to the Father except through me". Let's take a look at John's account:

<u>John 1:6-16</u>

6 There was a man sent from God, whose name was John. 7 This man came for a witness, to bear witness of the light, that all through him might believe. 8 He was not that Light, but was sent to bear witness of that Light. 9 That was the true Light which gives light to every man coming into the world. ***10 He was in the world, and the world was made through Him, and the world did not know Him.*** *11 He came to His own, and His own did not receive Him.* ***12 But as many as received Him, to them He gave the right to become children of God, to those who believe in His name****: 13 who were born, not of blood, nor of the will of the flesh, nor of the will of man, but of God. 14 And the Word became flesh and dwelt among us, and we beheld His glory, the glory as of the only begotten of the Father, full of grace and truth. 15 John bore witness of Him and cried out, saying, "This was He of whom I said, 'He who comes after me is preferred before me, for He was before me.' 16 And of His fullness we have all received, and grace for grace.*

<u>John 6:32-33</u>

32 Then Jesus said to them, "Most assuredly, I say to you, Moses did not give you the bread from heaven, but My Father gives you the true bread from heaven. ***33 For the bread of God is He who comes down from heaven and gives life to the world."***

John 7:14-15

[14] *Now about the middle of the feast Jesus went up into the temple and taught.* [15] ***And the Jews marveled, saying, "How does this Man know letters, having never studied?"***

John 16:15

[15] ***All things that the Father has are Mine****. Therefore I said that He will take of Mine and declare it to you.*

John 1:1-5

In the beginning was the Word, and the Word was with God, and the Word was God. [2] *He was in the beginning with God.* [3] ***All things were made through Him, and without Him nothing was made that was made.*** [4] *In Him was life, and the life was the light of men.* [5] *And the light shines in the darkness, and the darkness did not comprehend it.*

In the story of creation, God employed His Word to implement or execute His Will. When He concluded His thoughts, He spoke them and then they manifested; what was intangible became tangible and fully functioning. Jesus Christ is the Word of God made flesh. God wrapped His Word in flesh, He gave the Word actual physical form, but the mission of the Word remained the same, **Jesus Christ executed and executes the will of the Father**. The only word for this phenomenon is 'mystery' and that is exactly what the Apostle Paul refers to Jesus Christ as in Ephesians chapter 3. We will examine Ephesians after we form a more solid foundation from the following scriptures.

<u>John 8:28-59</u>

[28] Then Jesus said to them, "When you lift up the Son of Man, then you will know that I am He, and that I do nothing of Myself; but as My Father taught Me, I speak these things. [29] And He who sent Me is with Me. The Father has not left Me alone, for I always do those things that please Him."

<u>John 5:19-20, 36</u>

[9] Then Jesus answered and said to them, "Most assuredly, I say to you, the Son can do nothing of Himself, but what He sees the Father do; for whatever He does, the Son also does in like manner. [20] For the Father loves the Son, and shows Him all things that He Himself does; and He will show Him greater works than these, that you may marvel. [36] But I have a greater witness than John's; for the works which the Father has given Me to finish – the very works that I do – bear witness of Me, that the Father has sent Me.

<u>John 12:49-50</u>

For I have not spoken on My own authority; but the Father who sent Me gave Me a command, what I should say and what I should speak. **50** *And I know that His command is everlasting life. Therefore, whatever I speak, just as the Father has told Me, so I speak."*

John 7:16

16 *Jesus*[a] *answered them and said, "My doctrine is not Mine, but His who sent Me.*

3.4: THE REASON
Part II

John 3:34

*Jesus said to them, "My food is to do the will of Him who sent Me, **and to finish His work**.*

I was looking for a way not to include this whole chapter, but to really understand the power of the truth revealed in the passage of scripture we must read the whole thing.

Ephesians 3

*For this reason I, Paul, the prisoner of Christ Jesus for you Gentiles – [2] if indeed you have heard of the dispensation of the grace of God which was given to me for you, [3] how that by revelation He **made known to me the mystery** (as I have briefly written already, [4] by which, **when you read, you may understand my knowledge in the mystery of Christ**), [5] which in other ages was not made known to the sons of men, as it has now been revealed by the Spirit to His holy apostles and prophets: [6] that the Gentiles should be fellow heirs, of the same* *body, and partakers of His promise in Christ through the gospel,* [7] *of which I became a minister according to the gift of the grace of God given to me by the effective working of His power.*

(Purpose of the Mystery)

[8] *To me, who am less than the least of all the saints, this grace was given, that I should preach among the Gentiles the unsearchable riches of Christ,* [9] *and* ***to make all see what is the fellowship of the mystery, which from the beginning of the ages has been hidden in God who created all things through Jesus Christ;*** [10] ***to the intent that now the manifold wisdom of God might be made known by the church to the principalities and powers in the heavenly places,*** [11] ***according to the eternal purpose which He accomplished in Christ Jesus our Lord,*** [12] *in whom we have boldness and access with confidence through faith in Him.* [13] *Therefore I ask that you do not lose heart at my tribulations for you, which is your glory.*

(Appreciation of the Mystery)

[14] *For this reason I bow my knees to the Father* [f] *of our Lord Jesus Christ,* [15] *from whom the whole family in heaven and earth is named,* [16] *that He would grant you, according to the riches of His glory, to be strengthened with might through His Spirit in the inner man,* [17] *that Christ may dwell in your hearts through faith; that you, being rooted and grounded in love,* [18] *may be able to comprehend with all the saints what is the width and length and*

depth and height – [19] to know the love of Christ which passes knowledge; that you may be filled with all the fullness of God.

[20] Now to Him who is able to do exceedingly abundantly above all that we ask or think, according to the power that works in us, [21] to Him be glory in the church by Christ Jesus to all generations, forever and ever. Amen

I am going to attempt to be brief in my explanation of this text, but give fair warning it may be a little lengthy. Here we go… The main topic Paul is trying to communicate to believers in this passage of scripture is the **mystery of the power of the Word of God** and thus **the mystery of the power of Jesus Christ** in which believers (the Church) have fellowship. The word mystery is defined as something that is difficult or impossible to understand or explain. Believers in Ephesus were living and experiencing contrasting extremes. Imagine witnessing, winning souls for Christ and seeing miracles performed due to the power of God through His word, yet not seeing that same power deliver or spare you from enduring hardships brought upon you because you promoted God's cause. Under God's divine inspiration, Paul takes time to usher the church of Ephesus to a position of understanding the purpose and power of it all. Paul's explanation also would empower these new converted believers to grow in their comprehension of God.

The passage reveals understanding of the mystery of the Word of God, that had been hidden from the beginning of the ages until this revelatory explanation was shared. God used His intangible Word to initiate life on Earth and to impact (allow or restrict) activity within. With the birth of Jesus Christ, the once intangible Word of God became wrapped in the flesh of man, and now exists in tangible form. In the Old Testament Isaiah informs us about the Word's creative nature, being living and active even in the intangible form. In the New Testament the Word is now housed in Jesus Christ!

If we fast forward to the end of the passage, we come to understand God's will to do miraculous things through the individuals who allow this power of the Word to be at work in them. The conclusion of the passage encourages believers in God through Christ, to draw strength from the power of the Word and not lose heart, for they are enabled to wield its power in the Earth realm. Paul under divine inspiration was used by God to communicate to believers the potential of the Word of God when it is unleashed through our faith and correlating actions, as we go through various seasons of our lives, especially the turbulent or more challenging experiences.

Now, as if that wasn't enough revealed, God answers or reveals what I'm pretty sure every believer in times past, present and times yet to come, place in the their top five questions for God to answer: "God what is the purpose of it all?" and "God why are you playing this game with Satan and his followers? This answer can be found in Ephesians 3:10:

To the intent *that now the manifold wisdom of God* ***might be made known by the church to the principalities and powers in the heavenly places,*** *[11] according to the eternal purpose which He accomplished in Christ Jesus our Lord".*

This text reveals God is using the church to teach, display and confirm to the heavenly host the absolute power of His Word to orchestrate and deliver according to design.

3.5: HIS CURRENT POSITION & OCCUPATION

Romans 8:**31**

[31] What then shall we say to these things? If God is for us, who can be against us? [32] He who did not spare His own Son, but delivered Him up for us all, how shall He not with Him also freely give us all things? [33] Who shall bring a charge against God's elect? It is God who justifies. [34] Who is he who condemns? ***It is Christ who died, and furthermore is also risen, who is even at the right hand of God, who also makes intercession for us.***

I often wondered how Christ occupies his time in heaven. I know Christ is sitting at the right hand of God the Father, but what does he do as he awaits His triumphant second return. I did not often hear preachers shine light on the details regarding what He was doing. I found Romans 8:31-34 to be significant. This scripture sheds light on Jesus Christ current position and His partial function.

We should be exceedingly joyful Jesus Christ, our risen Savior is currently seated at the right hand of the Father with all power in His hands, awaiting His triumphant second return. To be placed at the right hand of a leader has significance. It is a position of honor denoting one to be an extension of their power and the point person or lead assistant entrusted to fulfill carrying out the leader's mission (purpose).

While waiting to fulfill the God's Word (plan) in entirety and usher us into 'life eternal', Jesus Christ makes intercession for us as Satan continually presents himself before God the Father to bring accusation and highlight the disobedience of believers. Believers are the bride of Christ as revealed in Ephesians chapter 5, and Christ gave his life for believers. In Jesus Christ we have a High Priest who understands and is able to relate to our infirmities as revealed in Hebrews 4. So, when Satan the accuser of the brethren comes with his list of truthful accusations, the sacrificial power of the love of Christ at Calvary renders the case to be dismissed for Christ himself intercedes on our behalf. This is another lift your hands and tell Christ thank you moment! God the Father looks at Christ and simply says, "Case dismissed".

Hebrews 4:14

[14] Seeing then that we have a great High Priest who has passed through the heavens, Jesus the Son of God, let us hold fast our confession. ***[15] For we do not have a High Priest who cannot sympathize with our weaknesses, but was in all points tempted as we are, yet without sin.*** *[16] Let us therefore come boldly to the throne of grace, that we may obtain mercy and find grace to help in time of need.*

Ephesians 1:19-21

[19] and what is the exceeding greatness of His power toward us who believe, according to the working of His mighty power [20] which He worked in Christ when He raised Him from the dead ***and seated Him at His right hand in the heavenly places, [21] far above all principality and power and might and dominion****, and every name that is named, not only in this age but also in that which is to come.*

Psalms 110:1

The LORD said to my Lord, "Sit at My right hand, till I make your enemies Your footstool."

Ephesians 5

[22] Wives, submit to your own husbands, as to the Lord. [23] For the husband is head of the wife, ***as also Christ is head of the church; and He is the Savior of the body****. [24] Therefore, just as the church is subject to Christ, so let the wives be to their own husbands in everything.* ***[25] Husbands, love your wives, just as***

Christ also loved the church and gave Himself for her, *[26] that He might [g]sanctify and cleanse her with the washing of water by the word.*

Romans 8:34

[34] Who is he who condemns? ***It is Christ who died, and furthermore is also risen, who is even at the right hand of God, who also makes intercession for us****.*

Colossians 3:1

If then you were raised with Christ, seek those things which are above, ***where Christ is, sitting at the right hand of God****.*

Satan is the accuser of the brethren!

Revelations 12:10

[10] Then I heard a loud voice saying in heaven, "Now salvation, and strength, and the kingdom of our God, and the power of His Christ have come, ***for the accuser of our brethren, who accused them before our God day and night****, has been cast down.*

Job 1:6

[6] Now there was a day when ***the sons of God came to present themselves before the LORD and Satan also came among them.***

3.6: I AM A BENEFICIARY

Jesus Christ says of Himself, that He is the way, He is the truth and the He is the life and that no one comes God the Father except through Him. Coming to God the Father completely and being connected to Him fully, requires belief in Jesus Christ. We are rendered incapable without coming by way of accepting the full testimony of Jesus Christ (origin, birth, life lived, death experience and resurrection). In the book of John, it is revealed by Jesus Christ that the Father seeks to be pursued, reverenced and served by dedicated believers (worshipped) in Spirit and in truth. To go a little farther, one is not capable of receiving the Holy Spirit's inward dwelling without accepting the full testimony of Jesus Christ.

Beneficiary is defined as a person or group that receives benefits, profits, or advantages. The title of this section is 'I Am A Beneficiary' because I want to close the discussion of Jesus Christ highlighting the benefits, profits or advantages of what belief entitles believers to; what it entitles me to. The primary benefit to being a beneficiary of the sacrifice of Jesus Christ through my belief is without a doubt is my soul escaping the penalty of life eternal in hell and gaining life eternal with God. However, it does not stop there! My belief in Jesus Christ makes me a beneficiary of living life on earth mortally or in the flesh not under the bondage of sin and the associated limitations of sin.

Jesus Christ stated His reason for coming included positioning us to not just live, but to have (live) life more abundantly. Abundantly is defined as present in great quantity; more than adequate; over-sufficient. Why should we merely live when we can live in abundance? 'Walking the line' to experience living life abundantly through Christ further positions us to secure our eternal seat with God.

John 10:7

[7] Then Jesus said to them again, "Most assuredly, I say to you, I am the door of the sheep. [8] All who ever came before Me are thieves and robbers, but the sheep did not hear them. [9] I am the door. If anyone enters by Me, he will be saved, and will go in and out and find pasture. [10] The thief does not come except to steal, and to kill, and to destroy. ***I have come that they may have life, and that they may have it more abundantly.***

John 10:15-18

[15] *As the Father knows Me, even so I know the Father;* ***and I lay down My life for the sheep.*** [16] ***And other sheep I have which are not of this fold; them also I must bring, and they will hear My voice; and there will be one flock and one shepherd.*** [17] *"Therefore My Father loves Me, because I lay down My life that I may take it again.* [18] *No one takes it from Me, but I lay it down of Myself. I have power to lay it down, and I have power to take it again. This command I have received from My Father."*

Romans 8:1

There is therefore now no condemnation to those who are in Christ Jesus*, who do* ***not*** *walk according to the flesh, but according to the Spirit.*

Romans 8:31

[31] *Then Jesus said to those Jews who believed Him, "If you abide in My word, you are My disciples indeed.* [32] ***And you shall know the truth, and the truth shall make you free."*** [33] *They answered Him, "We are Abraham's descendants, and have never been in bondage to anyone. How can You say, 'You will be made free'?"* [34] *Jesus answered them, "Most assuredly, I say to you, whoever commits sin is a slave of sin.* [35] *And a slave does not abide in the house forever, but a son abides forever.*

John 3:16

[16] *For God so loved the world that He gave His only begotten Son,* ***that whoever believes in Him should not perish but have everlasting life.*** [17] *For God did not send His Son into the world to condemn the world, but that the world through Him might be saved.* [18] ***"He who believes in Him is not condemned; but he who does not believe is condemned already, because he has not believed in the name of the only begotten Son of God.***

John 14:

[12] *"Most assuredly, I say to you, he who believes in Me, the works that I do he will do also; and greater works than these he will do, because I go to My Father.* [13] *And whatever you ask in My name, that I will do, that the Father may be glorified in the Son.* [14] *If you* [a]*ask anything in My name, I will do it.*

SEGMENT 4

God, the Holy Spirit

4.1: THE OCCUPANT WITHIN

I believe The Holy Spirit of God is the most misunderstood and unexplored counterpart of the Trinity. Growing up in a Pentecostal Church, I often heard the Holy Spirit referred to as the Holy Ghost. Just the word "ghost" being used in the description automatically made me see it through a mystical or spooky lens. I believe this rings true for many historically and presently. The word ghost sparks fear in some, due to the unknown. However, the Holy Spirit should not been seen through a scary lens at all. A believer should see the Holy Spirit as that best older friend to be appreciated and respected to the utmost, because the Holy Spirit is the main resource made available to believers, by

God the Father, via the request of Jesus Christ, to empower us.

Many people have relegated and minimized the function or purpose of the Holy Spirit to a physical exhibition, whereas to prove spirituality and this evidenced or made known by one speaking in unknown tongues. While speaking in tongues can be one of the outward displays of the inward dwelling of the Holy Spirit, it by far is not the sum total of the role of the Holy Spirit in the life of a believer. A few Christian denominations teach or suggest speaking in tongues to be 'thee,' as in only, evidence. I submit in love, I do not agree with this belief. Scripturally, the Holy Spirit and the Holy Ghost are one in the same. Evangelist Billy Graham, perhaps the most influential evangelist of the 20th Century stated, "The term Holy Spirit and Holy Ghost mean exactly the same thing… Remember the Holy Spirit is God Himself and He is at work both in the world and in our hearts".

We receive the Holy Spirit when we accept God's plan of salvation made available through Jesus Christ (i.e., confession verbally and belief inwardly). Based on this, I believe the Holy Spirit should be included in the foundational teaching of Christians of all ages, as it aids us in learning about:

- The character of God,
- The purpose of God,
- Our role within His purpose,
- The Written Word of God (properly interpreting it), and
- Living according to Kingdom standards.

Think about it, as Christian adults how much more fruitful would our lives be if we had been taught how to properly utilize and submit to the Holy Spirit, which provides counsel as we endeavor to learn about Elohim, the sovereign God, our Creator full of power. In the Gospel of John chapter 10, Jesus Christ stated, "I have come that they may have life and that they may have *it* more abundantly". The Holy Spirit leads us to the abundant life available. When preparing His disciples for His departure, that would be initiated by crucifixion and culminate with Him ascending to sit at the right hand of the Father (after His resurrection), Christ gave His disciples this assurance:

John 14:18

[18] I will not leave you orphans; I will come to you. *[19] "A little while longer and the world will see Me no more, but you will see Me. Because I live, you will live also. [20] At that day you will know that I am in My Father, and you in Me, and I in you.*

To secure abundant life for His disciples, Jesus Christ prayed to the Father on behalf His disciples (past, present and future -inclusive of the Body of Christ today; the Church) and requested that we be endowed and equipped with the Holy Spirit of God.

<u>John 14:16</u>

[16] ***And I will pray to the Father, and He will give you another Helper, that He may abide with you forever—*** [17] ***the Spirit of truth,*** *whom the world cannot receive, because it neither sees Him nor knows Him; but you know Him,* ***for He dwells with you and will be in you.***

This empowering request of Christ, to the Father positions disciples (followers) of Christ to have a Comforter and Counselor, capable of guiding us to experience life "more abundantly". This text contains life-changing promises for those who make the choice to love Christ. Our love for Christ (the Word of God made flesh) makes way for the Father to respond by making His home in us by way of the Holy Spirit. Again, imagine if our children were taught this and how to utilize the Holy Spirit at an early age; imagine if new converts of all ages submitted to being led by the Holy Spirit at the beginning of their journey. What if we really grasped the reality of the following text:

<u>John 14:21</u>

[21] *He who has My commandments and keeps them, it is he who loves Me.* ***And he who loves Me will be loved by My Father, and I will love him and*** [f]***manifest Myself to him."*** [22] *Judas (not Iscariot) said to Him, "Lord, how is it that You will manifest Yourself to us, and not to the world?"* [23] ***Jesus answered and said to him, "If anyone loves Me, he will keep My word; and My Father will love him, and We will come to him and make Our home with him.*** [24] *He who does not love Me does not keep My words; and the word which you hear is not Mine but the Father's who sent Me.*

This text advises us of the intention and promise of the Father and the Son to take residence in believers, by way of the Holy Spirit. To help bring out the meaning of this let's consider the following scripture:

<u>I Corinthians 19-20</u>

[19] *Or do you not know that your body is the temple of the Holy Spirit who is in you, whom you have from God, and you are not your own?* [20] *For you were bought at a price; therefore glorify God in your body and in your spirit, which are God's.*

The thought of God living in me is a both overwhelming and exciting at the same time. The reality of this makes me want to structure my life in a manner that positions me be an honorable host, while I understand nothing I do will make me worthy. For the Creator full of power to physically come for a visit every now and then is one thing, but to carry Him with me daily, twenty-four hours a day, seven days a week, this is something to heavily consider. This means there is not a move I make or more importantly a thought I process, in which I do not take God in Trinity 'along for the ride'. Think about it, God has an intimate view of how I deal with thoughts, desires, etc. The reality of this is indescribable.

I dread having visitors show up to my home unannounced and my house not in 'ready to entertain' condition. For most of us, when we are made aware visitors are coming, it causes us to prepare our homes to entertain. We tidy up based on the access that will be granted to the individuals coming to visit. For example, if an acquaintance is coming over, I know their access to my home will be limited to my first floor area, inclusive of the living room, dining room, kitchen and guest bathroom, thus I clean accordingly. I did not say I was right for not cleaning the entire house, I was just honest about how I cut corners at times or limit my preparation due to access restrictions. However, if any of my immediate family is coming, my mother, siblings, or nephews I understand their level of accessibility to my home is virtually unlimited. I know my immediate family will not hesitate to go beyond my first floor if a need or want requires it. When I know members of my immediate family are coming, I try to pick the whole house up, clean it and put it back down, especially if my mom is 'in the mix!'

To think of what I go through to entertain mere humans is really funny at times, but how have I prepared for the daily indwelling of the Holy Spirit of God, whose access I cannot limit? How have I prepared to entertain or host the Trinity daily? How have you prepared to entertain God in Trinity daily? For me, and I imagine a great number of others, the answer to this question makes us say 'ouch', shake our heads in shame or both.

With all of this talk about preparing for the inward dwelling of the Holy Spirit, I would remiss if I didn't highlight the prerequisite or qualifying 'if' to receiving the Holy Spirit revealed by Christ, in John 14:23. Here Christ advises our love for Him and our adhering to His word is what triggers or initiates this indwelling of the Trinity in our lives. I would like to emphasize genuinely loving Christ extends beyond having sincere appreciation for His sacrifice at Calvary. If we truly grasp the fact and accept the revelation that Jesus Christ is the Word of God made flesh, as revealed in the first chapter of the gospel of John, it should trigger our quest to fall in love with the Word (plan, purpose and way) of God. This positions believers to be in a position of agreement, which yields more fruitful results than mere submission.

If we consider love from the natural perspective, true love 'calls into action' our willingness to learn the one we love and correspondingly commit to them. The same applies spiritually regarding our love for God. If we love God, we position ourselves to learn Him and commit to His way. It is our responsibility to unlock the capability of the Holy Spirit within us, which then gives way for the Holy Spirit to flow through us. The Holy Spirit will guide us to unlocking 'It' in our lives if we allow. Let's examine the following scripture to learn the capability of the Holy Spirit.

John 16:12-15

[12] "I still have many things to say to you, but you cannot bear them now.[13] However, when ***He, the Spirit of truth, has come, He will guide you into all truth; for He will not speak on His own authority, but whatever He hears He will speak; and He will tell you things to come.*** *[14] He will glorify Me, for He will take of what is Mine and declare it to you.*

What an awesome promise contained in this scripture for the qualified believer. For the Father to be willing to allow the Spirit of Truth, the Holy Spirit to share high-level conversations in the heavens with Christ disciples exemplifies His love for us. Access to this information gives Christ disciples distinct advantages. Armed with information from the throne of God, Christ disciples are able to adjust and prepare on a level that others cannot comprehend, fathom, understand or take advantage of. However, again I suggest we must be ushered to a place of being in 'agreement with' God, which requires submission.

Agreement is defined in the Oxford Dictionary as **the absence of incompatibility (mismatch, conflict, discordancy) between two things**. The Collins dictionary defines agreement to be **a formal decision about future action that is made between two or more parties**. Surprisingly, in many of the definitions describing submission, agreement is used in some tense (agreeing, agreement). I would like to offer my opinion that at its core submission does not always equate to being in agreement. I believe this because I can submit to something I absolutely do not agree with. For this reason, I will use the definition of submission offered by dictionary.com (slightly altered by me), **submission is defined as acting in obedience, particularly to a master**.

I submit that the Holy Spirit is the only tool we can depend on to guide us to a position of being in agreement with God vs. merely submitting to God. I believe many are serving God from a bitter and resentful place of submission.

I also believe that any one of us can subconsciously slip into this place. Where can this lead to? This leads us to a place of limitation and disconnection as it relates our relationship with God and being available for use. Christ describes the Holy Spirit as a Comforter as well as a Counselor. In order for us to remain in a position of being in divine alignment (consistently in line with the will of God and open to be used by God) we must depend on the Holy Spirit to counsel us to a place of comfort as we deal with what God allows and blocks in our lives.

Do we really comprehend the gift of the Holy Spirit? Have we really positioned ourselves to see the power of the Holy Spirit released in our lives? Are we having high-level conversations and consulting sessions with the Holy Spirit, or is the Holy Spirit like one of the gifts we have previously received, the one have left unwrapped, or never used to its full capacity? What is the gift inside of us?

4.2: THE POWER OF THE DEPOSIT

We have discussed how we receive the Holy Spirit and how important I believe the Holy Spirit is in our lives briefly. However, we have not discussed or described what the Holy Spirit that dwells within us actually is. Please consider a few questions to help open your mind and get 'the wheels turning.'

1. How would you describe the Holy Spirit of God?
2. Can we have a relationship with something we do not understand?
3. Can we be comfortable letting something lead us, not knowing how it operates, flows, or empowers?

Let's explore a few scriptures to help us lay a proper foundation.

<u>Revelation 1:4</u>

[4] John, to the seven churches which are in Asia: Grace to you and peace from Him who is and who was and who is to come (the Father), ***and from the seven Spirits who are before His throne (the Holy Spirit)****, [5] and from Jesus Christ (the Son), the faithful witness, the firstborn from the dead, and the ruler over the kings of the earth.*

From Revelations we see the Holy Spirit of God depicted, described, or embodied as seven Spirits before the throne. The number seven (7) is widely accepted biblically as the number of completeness or perfection. Is it possible that the significance of the number seven is foundationally based on there being seven attributes of the Holy Spirit? What does each one of the seven Spirits that account for the Holy Spirit of God represent or personify? Let's explore the book of Isaiah to answer this. The text below refers to the lineage of Jesus Christ, but also gives a description of the Spirit of God that was going to rest upon Him. Let's see what we can extract from the text.

<u>Isaiah 11:1</u>

There shall come forth a rod from the stem of Jesse, and a Branch shall grow out of his roots. [2] The Spirit of the LORD shall rest upon Him. The Spirit of wisdom and understanding, the Spirit of counsel and might, the Spirit of knowledge and of the fear of the LORD.

From the text we deduce that the seven Spirits that are synonymous with the Holy Spirit of God transferable to man are:

1. The Spirit of the Lord = the Spirit of Truth (John 14:6; 14:15-17),
2. The Spirit of Wisdom,
3. The Spirit of Understanding,
4. The Spirit of Counsel,
5. The Spirit of Might,
6. The Spirit of Knowledge, and
7. The Spirit of the Fear of Lord = the Spirit of reverence, honor (Psalms 103:17, 111:10).

To help us grasp the concept of the Spirit of Truth and the Spirit of Fear, in proper context and application, I offer these scriptures. Concerning the Spirit of Truth, Jesus said the following:

John 14:6

I am *the way, the truth and the life, No one comes to the father except through me.*

John 14:15-17

[15] *"If you love Me,* [a]*keep My commandments.* [16] *And I will pray the Father, and* ***He will give you another*** [b]***Helper, that He may abide with you forever—*** [17] ***the Spirit of truth****, whom the*

world cannot receive, because it neither sees Him nor knows Him; but you know Him, for He dwells with you and will be in you.

Psalms 138:1-2

I will praise You with my whole heart; before the gods I will sing praises to You. [2] I will worship toward Your holy temple, and praise Your name For Your lovingkindness and Your truth; ***For You have magnified Your word above all Your name****.*

Christ identifies the Holy Spirit as the Spirit of Truth that will abide with the believer forever. In speaking of Himself, the Word of God made flesh, Jesus reveals that He, the Word of God, is in fact truth. David indicates in Psalms that God Himself has the upmost reverence for what He says. How powerful is this considering He's God and does not have to. While God can do what He wants, how He wants, when He wants, yet he will not because He magnifies or reverences His Word above His name, identity and ability. In simple terms, God recognizes or has set it up so that He can be judged based on Him being a God of His Word. This might explain why such a high value is placed on truth in the Kingdom of God.

Concerning fear, the following texts are offered:

Proverbs 9:10

[10] The fear of the LORD is the beginning of wisdom,
And the knowledge of the Holy One is understanding.

Matthew 10:27

[27] "Whatever I tell you in the dark, speak in the light; and what you hear in the ear, preach on the housetops. [28] And do not fear those who kill the body but cannot kill the soul. But rather fear Him who is able to destroy both soul and body in [a]hell.

Psalms 111:10

The fear of the LORD is the beginning of wisdom; a good understanding have all those who do His commandments. His praise endures forever.

II Timothy 1:7

[7] For God has not given us a spirit of fear, but of power and of love and of a sound mind.

From these four passages, we see evidence of healthy fear as it pertains to God, which is reverent fear of God. II Timothy brings balance and points out that fear outside reverent fear of God is assigned by God and thus not profitable. Psalms 138:1-2, points out that God reverences

His Word above His name. In short, God chose to stake His identity on His Word. Based on the system He established, going against or outside of His word, would make Him a God with inconsistencies and broken promises and thus unjust. The commitment of God to His word is nothing short of amazing. Knowing God's Word that remains living and active, is vital in the life of a believer. The Devil knows the Word of God, he was there when some of it was written or established. Based on this he employs the Balaam strategy of getting God's people to go against His Word to stifle and prohibit the progression of believers (Numbers 22). The Bible further confirms this by advising us that God's own perish due to lack of knowledge (Hosea 4:6).

When we receive the Holy Spirit of God, it comes possessing and depositing all seven of God's attributes into us. We must learn to grow in them; to experience their fullness in our everyday lives though our daily routines.

We should also explore the passages in II Corinthians and Romans concerning the Spirit and gifts entrusted to man.

I Corinthians 12: 4

There are diversities of gifts, ***but the same Spirit****.* [5] *There are differences of ministries, but the same Lord.* [6] *And there are* *diversities of activities, but it is the same God who works all in all.* [7] ***But the manifestation of the Spirit is given to each one for the profit of all:*** [8] *for to one is given the word of* ***wisdom*** *through the Spirit, to another the* ***word of knowledge*** *through the same Spirit,* [9] *to another* ***faith*** *by the same Spirit, to another gifts of* ***healings*** *by the same Spirit,* [10] *to another the* ***working of miracles****, to another* ***prophecy****, to another* ***discerning of spirits****, to another* ***different kinds of tongues****, to another the* ***interpretation of tongues****.* [11] *But one and the same Spirit works all these things, distributing to each one individually as He wills.*

The manifestation of the inward dwelling of the Holy Spirit has the ability to activate gifts or abilities that are given for the primary purpose of profiting all mankind, not for our individual personal gain from exercising or flowing in the area of gifting. Our personal gain is secondary and should not be considered if we desire to keep our motive pure. Many are guilty of hijacking the gifts' purpose for their own personal gain, gratification, promotion, etc. The manifestation of the inward dwelling of the Holy Spirit, evidenced though disbursement of gifts, are to be used to bring glory to God.

Based upon the scriptures presented thus far, I believe the Holy Spirit of God is synonymous with the essence (substance, core) of God, as it is the intrinsic, all-encompassing, transferable power of God downloaded and manifested in those who believe in God, through Christ. The Oxford Dictionary defines essence as the intrinsic (innate, fundamental, built-in) nature or indispensable quality of something, especially something abstract that determines its character. For the believer, the Holy Spirit also functions as a liaison, as it connects the believer with God intimately. The Merriam Webster dictionary defines liaison as a person who helps organizations or groups to work together and provide information to each other. We must learn to utilize, respect and be led by the Holy Spirit to unlock the abundant life available to us through Christ. Let's look at the following text to support this theory.

<u>Ephesians 3:14-20</u>

[14] For this reason I bow my knees to the Father of our Lord Jesus Christ, [15] from whom the whole family in heaven and earth is named, [16] ***that He would grant you, according to the riches of His glory, to be strengthened with might through His Spirit in the inner man,*** *[17] that Christ may dwell in your hearts through faith; that you, being rooted and grounded in love, [18]* ***may be able to comprehend*** *with all the saints what is the width and length and depth and height – [19] to know the love of Christ which passes knowledge;* ***that you may be filled with all the fullness of God. [20] Now to Him who is able to do exceedingly***

abundantly above all that we ask or think, according to the power that works in us…

God is willing to use us to a greater degree, reveal to us in greater measures and usher us to abundant life, according to how we unlock the Holy Spirit through our spiritual maturation.

Let's add another layer to really grasp the capability of the Holy Spirit. The Holy Spirit gives us wisdom, which is the Holy Spirit's possession and thus grants access, so where the Holy Spirit is wisdom abounds. I believe Solomon was inspired to pen the words of the Holy Spirit in Proverbs chapter 8. Let's thoroughly explore this teaching.

Proverbs 8

*Does not wisdom cry out, And understanding lift up her voice? [2] She takes her stand on the top of the high hill, beside the way, where the paths meet. [3] She cries out by the gates, at the entry of the city, at the entrance of the doors: [4] "**To you, O men, I call, and my voice is to the sons of men.** [5] O you simple ones, understand prudence, and you fools, be of an understanding heart. [6] **Listen, for I will speak of excellent things, and from the opening of my lips will come right things; [7] For my mouth will speak truth; wickedness is an abomination to my lips.** [8] All the words of my mouth are with righteousness; nothing crooked or perverse is in them. [9] They are all plain to him who* *understands, and right to those who find knowledge.* [10] ***Receive my instruction**, and not silver, and knowledge rather than choice gold;* [11] *For wisdom is better than rubies, And all the things one may desire cannot be compared with her.* [12] *"**I, wisdom**, dwell with prudence, and find out knowledge and discretion.* [13] *The fear of the LORD is to hate evil; Pride and arrogance and the evil way and the perverse mouth I hate.* [14] ***Counsel is mine, and sound wisdom; I am understanding, I have strength.*** [15] *By me kings reign, and rulers decree justice.* [16] *By me princes rule, and nobles, All the judges of the earth.* [17] ***I love those who love me, and those who seek me diligently will find me.*** [18] *Riches and honor are with me, enduring riches and righteousness.* [19] ***My fruit is better than gold**, yes, than fine gold, and my revenue than choice silver.* [20] *I traverse the way of righteousness, In the midst of the paths of justice,* [21] *That I may cause those who love me to inherit wealth, That I may fill their treasuries.*

[22] ***"The LORD possessed me at the beginning of His way, before His works of old.*** [23] ***I have been established from everlasting, from the beginning, before there was ever an earth.*** [24] *When there were no depths I was brought forth, When there were no fountains abounding with water.* [25] *Before the mountains were settled, before the hills, I was brought forth;* [26] *While as yet He had not made the earth or the fields, Or the primal dust of the world.* [27] *When He prepared the heavens, I was there, When He drew a circle on the face of the deep,* [28] *When He established the clouds above, When He strengthened the*

fountains of the deep, [29] When He assigned to the sea its limit, So that the waters would not transgress His command, When He marked out the foundations of the earth, [30] ***Then I was beside Him as a master craftsman; And I was daily His delight, rejoicing always before Him, [31] Rejoicing in His inhabited world, and my delight was with the sons of men. [32] "Now therefore, listen to me, my children, for blessed are those who keep my ways. [33] Hear instruction and be wise, and do not disdain it. [34] Blessed is the man who listens to me, watching daily at my gates, waiting at the posts of my doors. [35] For whoever finds me finds life, and obtains favor from the LORD; [36] <u>But he who sins against me wrongs his own soul</u>; All those who hate me love death."***

I believe this chapter describes the overall, overarching function and potential power of the Holy Spirit in the life of the believer totally submitted. God desires to reveal Himself to us through the Holy Spirit as we develop a maturing relationship with Him. Verse 22 highlights the Holy Spirit of God was there with the Father from the beginning, before the Father's works of old. Verse 30 lets us know the Holy Spirit was present at the foundation of God's creative genius. Can we ask for a better guide to position us to understand God and His purposes? He was there when God started and added layer upon layer and precept upon precept. Let's get confirmation from Genesis.

<u>Genesis 1:</u>

In the beginning *God created the heavens and the earth.* [2] *The earth was without form, and void; and darkness* [a]*was on the face of the deep.* ***And the Spirit of God was hovering over the face of the waters.***

4.3: IT CAME BEARING FRUIT

Could we ask for a more considerate or thoughtful Creator, whose matchless love makes Him translate as Father? He has equipped the believer with an internal 'road map' and compass via the Holy Spirit, our 24 hour, 7 days a week internal Counselor and Comforter. Wow! The Holy Spirit serves as the advisor that has the potential to lead us to Godly change within. Proverbs 8:9 states, "My fruit is better than gold…" When God responds to the request of Jesus Christ and deposits the Holy Spirit, the essence of Himself (truth, wisdom, counsel, might, knowledge, understanding and reverent fear) it causes internal change. When the believer becomes spiritually impregnated with the Holy Spirit, it activates spiritual gifts and yields the Fruit of the Spirit. As we grow in God, the Fruit of the Spirit begins to grow within, budding and emerging. As the Fruit of the Spirit grows, it fills the space formerly occupied by the negative fruit and associated traits birthed by our flesh, that we rid ourselves of daily, as we go through the process of sanctification that was triggered by our salvation. The emergence of the Fruit of the Spirit aids us in combating the sin nature that prevailed when we were led by our flesh. As we grow in God, the Fruit of the Spirit gives way to correlating behavior changes, which is the ultimate evidence of the internal transformation sparked by the indwelling of the Holy Spirit. Transforming into the image of Christ, or living according to way of Christ, allows us to exude God the Father and serve as His ambassadors. The Bible teaches that we shall know a tree by its fruit (Matthew 7:15-20). Let's explore a few scriptures to gain support or evidence regarding transformation:

<u>Galatians 5:1-23</u>

[1]Stand fast therefore in the liberty by which Christ has made us free, and do not be entangled again with a yoke of bondage.

[16] I say then: ***Walk in the Spirit, and you shall not fulfill the lust of the flesh. [17] For the flesh lusts against the Spirit, and the Spirit against the flesh****; and these are contrary to one another, so that you do not do the things that you wish. [18] But if you* ***are led by the Spirit****, you are not under the law. [19] Now the works of the flesh are evident, which are: adultery, fornication, uncleanness, lewdness, [20] idolatry, sorcery, hatred, contentions, jealousies, outbursts of wrath, selfish ambitions, dissensions, heresies, [21] envy, murders, drunkenness, revelries, and the like; of which I tell you beforehand, just as I also told you in time past,*

that those who practice such things will not inherit the kingdom of God.

[22] ***But the fruit of the Spirit is love, joy, peace, longsuffering, kindness, goodness, faithfulness,*** [23] ***gentleness and self-control. Against such things there is no law.***

II Corinthians 5:17

[17] *Therefore if any man be in Christ, he is a new creature: old things are passed away; behold, all things are become new.*

Romans 7:19

[19] *For the good that I will to do, I do not do; but the evil I will not to do, that I practice.* [20] *Now if I do what I will not to do, it is no longer I who do it, but sin that dwells in me.* [21] *I find then a law, that evil is present with me, the one who wills to do good.* [22] *For I delight in the law of God according to the inward man.* [23] ***But I see another law in my members, warring against the law of my mind, and bringing me into captivity to the law of sin which is in my members.*** [24] *O wretched man that I am! Who will deliver me from this body of death?* [25] *I thank God – through Jesus Christ our Lord!*

God, in His exhibition of unmerited mercy and disbursement of overcoming grace does not expect us to change without Him, He knows better. Thus, the Holy Spirit, the 'gift that keeps on giving', enables and empowers us to transform as we continuously go through the process of sanctification (growing in the divine empowerment of God, shedding negative characteristics, habits, etc., and taking on ways of holiness in order to be set apart for particular use in a special purpose or work). Please allow me to note, it is referred to as the fruit of the Spirit not the fruits of the Spirit. The take away here is, the deposit of the Holy Spirit yields all nine fruits and each should be active in our lives as we submit to the will and way of God. God's desire is for us to develop overall, not just in certain areas.

4.4: CAUTION! HANDLE WITH CARE

In Proverbs 8:36, another alarming truth is revealed that we must look at and examine closely. The ramifications of being ignorant to this have severe penalties, even unto death.

Proverbs 8:36

But he who sins against me wrongs his own soul; all those who hate me love death."

What exactly does this verse imply and bring to light? This verse indicates that that whoever goes against the counsel or wisdom of the Holy Spirit is causing injury to themselves, an injury that leads to death. In addition, those who develop a hatred for the work and things pertaining to the Holy Spirit guarantee certain death for themselves. To help bring out the severity of this, let's get the Father's perspective or judgement regarding mishandling the Holy Spirit.

Matthew 12

[25] *But Jesus knew their thoughts, and said to them: "***Every kingdom divided against itself is brought to desolation***, and every city or house divided against itself will not stand.* [26] *If Satan casts out Satan, he is divided against himself. How then will his kingdom stand?* [27] *And if I cast out demons by Beelzebub, by whom do your sons cast them out? Therefore they shall be your judges.* [28] *But if I cast out demons by the Spirit of God, surely the kingdom of God has come upon you.* [29] *Or how can one enter a strong man's house and plunder his goods, unless he first binds the strong man? And then he will plunder his house.* [30] *He who is not with Me is against Me, and he who does not gather with Me scatters abroad.*

[31] ***"Therefore I say to you, every sin and blasphemy will be forgiven men, but the blasphemy against the Spirit will not be forgiven men.*** [32] ***Anyone who speaks a word against the Son of Man, it will be forgiven him; but whoever speaks against the Holy Spirit, it will not be forgiven him, either in this age or in the age to come.***

Mark 3:28-29

[28] *"Assuredly, I say to you, all sins will be forgiven the sons of men, and whatever blasphemies they may utter;* [29] *but he who blasphemes against the Holy Spirit never has forgiveness, but is subject to eternal condemnation"*

Let's consider the gravity of the text. The text says you can speak a word against the Son of God, who died on the cross for humanity, but if you speak against or blaspheme the Holy Spirit, you will never be forgiven, today or in the future. The word blaspheme is defined in the Merriam Webster Dictionary as the act of insulting or showing contempt (disrespect, hatred, dislike) or lack of reverence for God. The text above makes clear the consequences of this are fatal. Have we really viewed our actions and thoughts through this lens? Are we cautious regarding how we handle or regard God's Holy Spirit within? This is a serious question to consider.

There is grave danger in this reality, due to the tendency of mankind to take issue with anything or anyone who does not agree with, support, condone or dares to challenge our actions. For the believer, the Holy Spirit is our compass. So, when we are making decisions and leaning toward the way of error, it is the Holy Spirit that convicts and gives us the 'beware danger ahead' signal. For those 'on the fence' or struggling in the area of submission, there is great potential for the Holy Spirit becoming a nuisance and this can lead to dislike and contempt toward the gift given to help us. Matthew 6:24 advises that we cannot successfully serve two masters, that over the course of time the one practicing this behavior will come to love one and hate the other.

To really process the gravity placed on this, I had to really consider scripturally what God hates. What God hates in scripture is described as an abomination, a sin. In cases of those practicing abominable things, God takes his hands off you and turns you over to yourself, without His intervention. An abomination is a sin that perverts, twists or distorts God's truth or intent. For an example, lying is an abominable sin because it goes against truth. Another example can be found in looking at the sin of fornication vs. the sin of homosexuality. God dislikes fornication because it practices what God ordained to be out of timing or out of the covenant of marriage. So sex is not a sin, God created it, but it is to be practiced within God-established parameters. Homosexuality is sex with one of the same gender. This goes against the intent, design and purpose of God, thus it is on the list of what God hates, because it is a perversion. If we process blasphemy through this lens or standard, perhaps God weighs blasphemy more severely because it is creation speaking against the actual Creator, it is creation consciously making a conscious decision to refuse God's empowerment, so God notes and honors your refusal.

We would do well to remember the Holy Spirit is consistently with us. We certainly do not want to be found guilty of blaspheming the Holy Spirit. The penalty of being guilty of blasphemy is more than we will be able to bear.

The Conclusion

I would like to thank you for embarking on this journey to unlock the power of the Trinity in our lives. I truly believe the foundational biblical truths expressed in this book serve as a literal survival guide. It is my prayer that your knowledge and understanding that we are being sustained in the moment in time and prepared for tomorrow by the will of the Father, because of the Jesus Christ and with the Holy Spirit has been enhanced. I pray that we exhibit wisdom with the knowledge and understanding God has made available to us. The value of your support, of the commission of God on my life is beyond expression of words.

Please be on the lookout for my next book to be released in the last quarter of 2021, 'The Revelation: The Mystery Unfolded'. This book is special to me, because it is a collaboration of a sort, between my father, Minister Charles E. Stewart, who transitioned to be with the Lord, and myself. God impressed upon him to prepare believers for the 2nd coming of Jesus Christ, by sharing and helping others understand the 'prophetic roadmap' released to us in the book of Revelation.

In addition, and certainly not least, I encourage you to get your copy of '**Selah'**, words of inspiration from myself packaged as a daily empowerment tool, by author Douglas Harris. This book is available now! God impressed upon Pastor Harris to gather excerpts of five years of inspirational teachings and package them as an empowerment tool for believers. I am honored that Pastor Harris consented to the voice of God and dedicated his time and resources to deliver this tool of daily empowerment into your hands.

About the Author

Pastor Damian C. Stewart was raised in a God-fearing home by his parents Minister Charles E. Stewart and Elder Sharon M. Stewart. Together they lived according to the Word of God and instilled it in him. Pastor Stewart notes his unique spiritual composition to come from his father being a 'student of the Word' or a 'teacher's teacher', and his mother being a fiery preacher and exhorter of the Word and prayer warrior with a prophetic mantle. The family's membership at Rock of Ages Holy Church, under the pastorate of Bishop Raymond Walker, Jr. provided a firm foundation of 'holiness being a lifestyle' and inspired his pursuit for God's truth at an early age.

Rock of Ages' Music Department had a rare and powerful anointing, which allowed the gift of music ministry within him to be birthed and cultivated. Pastor Stewart's musical gifts were influenced at Rock of Ages by Kevin Walker, Pastor Darrell Parham Sr., Nate Bandy, and Eugene Moore. Pastor Stewart's musical gifts were first shared outside of the local assembly, as a musician of the John Bartram High School Choir under the leadership of Dr. Joanne Bailey, where he would meet and be further influenced musically by Zakery Williams. God continued to open doors allowing his passion for music ministry and leadership to be shared. He played for the Eastern College Angels of Harmony, Kutztown University Gospel Choir and Temple University Gospel Choir. Through the years, Pastor Stewart has helped many churches, from various denominations, build their music departments to the glory of God.

With each musical opportunity God cultivated and ignited Pastor Stewart's thirst for evangelism. God strategically allowed his musical gifts to position him to serve and observe powerful men and women of God. The growing hunger for evangelism caused Pastor Stewart to challenge Temple's Gospel Choir to not only sing, but to provide platforms for evangelism and service. This paved the way for Pastor Stewart to establish the Kingdom Works Coalition. This ministry targeted college students and young adults and is well known throughout the East Coast for hosting Church on Campus and the College Fest Conferences for over ten years.

In 1999, Pastor Stewart joined Oasis of Refreshing Ministries under the pastorate of Bishop Bruce V. Parham. The radical side of Pastor Stewart was strengthened as Bishop Parham taught members to "keep your own flavor" and "dare to be different." Under Bishop Parham, in 2001, Pastor Stewart was submitted, licensed and released to minister the Gospel by Bishop Ralph Dennis of Kingdom Fellowship Covenant Ministries. In 2004, Pastor Stewart joined Covenant House of God, under the pastorate of Apostle Hagans, where ironically her strengths were in his areas of weakness.

Pastor Stewart faced a problem with each evangelistic endeavor. He developed a burden for the souls that were won, rededicated and/or encouraged to become mature Christians. This caused Pastor Stewart to seek God to answer the question, why? God's answer was surprising and life-changing. In 2007, answering the call of God Pastor Stewart founded Kingdom Worship Center Church, Inc., a non-denominational ministry with a mission to empower people to new levels of freedom in God, through maturing faith, instant obedience and consistent action.

Today, his quest is "to maximize every opportunity and minimize his misses", by observing and living according to the Word of God, while hearing and responding to the voice of God. God has placed a mandate on Pastor Stewart to release literary works to empower the people of God, by outlining His truths as directed. In addition, Pastor Stewart established Fluent Music Group,

Inc. in 2018, a company endeavoring to produce empowering music through collaborative efforts. With his queen, Keena Stewart and his children, Diore, Bryce, Nia and Sanai by his side, he endeavors to 'unpack' what God has placed inside of him.

Made in the USA
Middletown, DE
30 January 2021